In the Web
of Ideas

Also By Charles Scribner, Jr.

Author:

In the Company of Writers: A Life in Publishing

The Devil's Bridge (children's book, illustrated by
Evaline Ness)

"Henri Poincaré and the Theory of Relativity," *American
Journal of Physics* (1964)

Scientific Imagery in Proust," *Proceedings of the American
Philosophical Society* (1990)

Translator:

Hansel und Gretel by the Brothers Grimm
(illustrated by Adrienne Adams)

Doppelfinten by Gabriel Laub

Le Jardin du Sphinx by Pierre Berloquin

Editor:

The Enduring Hemingway

The Complete Short Stories of Ernest Hemingway

In the Web
of Ideas

The Education of a Publisher

CHARLES SCRIBNER, JR.

Introduction by
Charles Scribner III

CHARLES SCRIBNER'S SONS
NEW YORK

Charles Scribner's Sons
Macmillan Publishing Company
866 Third Avenue, New York, NY 10022
Collier Macmillan Canada, Inc.

Library of Congress Cataloging-in-Publication Data
Scribner, Charles, 1921–
In the web of ideas: the education of a publisher / Charles Scribner, Jr.;
introduction by Charles Scribner III.
p. cm.
ISBN 978-1-5011-1243-0

1. Scribner, Charles, 1921– . 2. Publishers and publishing—
United States—Biography. 3. Charles Scribner's Sons—
History—20th century. 4. Authors and publishing—United States—
History—20th century. I. Title.
Z473.S392 1993
070.5'092—dc20
[B]   92-40788   CIP

Macmillan books are available at special discounts for bulk purchases
for sales promotions, premiums, fund-raising, or education use.
For details, contact:

Special Sales Director
Macmillan Publishing Company
866 Third Avenue
New York, NY 10022

10 9 8 7 6 5 4 3 2 1
Printed in the United States of America

Once again, to my wife, Joan,
whose love and support
enrich every page;
and to our three sons—
Charles, Blair, and John

Contents

Preface

Reflecting upon the lifetime I have devoted to reading, writing, and publishing, I would have to say that my guiding principle has been a conviction articulated by the great physicist Josiah Willard Gibbs. He believed that the principal object of theoretical research in any department of knowledge was to find the point of view from which the subject appeared in its greatest simplicity.

All my life I have been motivated by intellectual curiosity often combined with a passion for theory. As a schoolboy I was introduced to the philosophical writings of William James, and though most of these were far over my head, the effort to get my mind around them served as a philosophical exercise in clear thinking and graceful writing. Looking back on my early readings and intellectual ambitions, I have sometimes felt like Virgil's Aeneas at the time his mother, Venus, presented him with a glorious new shield. All the major events in the future history of Rome had been carved on the face. Aeneas did not have the slightest idea what those prophetic scenes meant, but he was sure that they were terribly important.

It was these early readings that paved the road for the house that Scribners became under my leadership. When I joined Scribners, we were a new team that benefited at once by a number of best-sellers that had already been signed up, including books by Charles Lindbergh, Alan Paton, and a smash best-seller entitled *Not as a Stranger,* by Morton Thompson. But as the years went by, the sales of books we were publishing for bookstores were not holding up as they should. Puzzled by this, I finally came to the conclusion that we had become too much enthralled by our past and too exclusively committed to the publication of novels as compared with other genres. We were trying to carry on the marvelous successes of Maxwell Perkins in discovering new talent, but competition in the industry had grown immensely, and as a result our editors were signing up new writers on the promise of talent rather than talent itself.

Finally, I made a conscious decision to branch out into many other fields of publishing to which we had paid comparatively little attention in previous years. This included books in science, history, medicine, gardening, and a variety of crafts and hobbies. I was greatly aided in my quest for new titles by our director of trade publishing, Jack Galazka, who eventually became president of Charles Scribner's Sons. The literary agents looked at us somewhat critically as we were able to find books on our own—without their help. It was when I discovered this way to link my career as a book publisher with my varied interests as a book reader that life became enormously more interesting. My creativity as an editor and publisher soared.

Nowhere did my readings serve me more fully than in the development of the reference book program. Although the *Dictionary of American Biography* had been well received, the set offered no room for my creativity. It was in the formulation of the *Dictionary of Scientific Biography* and the *Dictionary of the History of Ideas* that I began to pump new life into the Scribner line while simultaneously broadening the scope of reference book publishing in general.

An underlying aim of all Scribner reference books has been to present a subject in its greatest simplicity so it will be clear to all levels of readers. As a means of interpreting the abstract theories I have encountered in my own readings, I have since childhood always recorded these ideas and pared them down to their essence, as far as practicable. By doing so I have often crystallized my understanding of a subject. Once when I was laid up in the infirmary at St. Paul's School with the mumps, I composed what I hoped would be interesting essays for my roommates. I remember feeling rewarded that they enjoyed what I had written.

In my adult life my readings have enabled me to become an essayist and speaker. One of my first speeches was to a ladies' church club in Gladstone, New Jersey, and the success of this speech on my longstanding interest in the English language led to its publication in the local newspaper. In 1966 I was invited to give a talk for the Classical League in Bowling Green, Kentucky, on the enduring value of the Greek and Roman classics. That was the first lecture I gave in the field. Shortly after that I began writing for the Princeton University magazine on a variety of intellectual topics.

These and other venues have allowed me to present sophisticated ideas I was reading about in a simpler form to larger audiences. I have selected for inclusion in this book—a fusion of memoir and ideas—a number of my writings about language, literature, books, and science, as well as some general observations on the vicissitudes of daily life. Based upon a life-

CHARLES SCRIBNER, JR.

time spent pursuing endeavors that could enrich the life of the mind, the various essays that constitute this book convey many of my most enduring convictions about reading, writing, and scholarship.

Acknowledgments

I wish to express special thanks to the following people who made this book possible. To my son Charlie, who commissioned it and kept it on course; to my longtime colleague and friend Jacques Barzun, who with literary perfect pitch fine tuned every page; to the gifted and equally indefatigable publisher of Scribner Reference and Twayne, Karen Day, whom I now can proudly claim as my own publisher; to my talented researcher and editor, Ann Leslie Tuttle, who improved it in countless ways from preparing the original typescript to shepherding it through each stage of publication; and to my assistants, Lisa Griffith and Thomas Slaboda, who were always as cheerful as helpful in my new career as a writer. Special thanks are also due to copy editor Barbara Sutton, proofreader David Hall, designers Erich Hobbing and Blake Logan, art director Lisa Chovnick, and production director Theresa Dieli. Finally, my wife Joan, has earned much more than the dedication: it provides but a glimmer of the debt I so gratefully acknowledge.

Introduction

This book has two parents—my own. My father authored it over the past twenty-five years; in recent months, my mother promoted it into print. His 1990 publishing memoir *In the Company of Writers* drew the sincerest of all praise from friends and colleagues—the simple question: "When is your next book due?" My mother religiously relayed its every repetition to me at Scribners, with the result that I soon plunged into a box I had been keeping in my office. It contained a quarter-century's worth of my father's speeches and essays on a variety of topics, all related to books and more generally to what he likes to call "the life of the mind." These were supplemented—enriched and seasoned—by a year-and-a-half's worth of weekly pieces composed for Malcolm Forbes's New Jersey newspaper, the *Hills-Bedminster Press*, which my mother, his scribe for many of the dictated columns, had collected and saved—as much for a second life in print as for posterity. Revised and arranged thematically, these essays have been a delight to reread in their final setting, revealing an intellectual structure that seems at once organic and architectural. The author's own title best sums them up: a *web of ideas*. When I asked him how he saw himself therein ("Are you the spider or the fly?"), his response was deliberately Delphic: he declined to be pinned down.

This past summer I spent several pleasant days at work sorting family and publishing files bound for the Scribner Archives at the Princeton University Library. I suppose it was this task as much as any latent nostalgia that prompted me to clean out my own storage boxes of letters, press clippings, and other memorabilia. In the process I came upon a small treasure that makes my assignment of introducing this volume all the easier: a bundle of letters from my father to me at a New England boarding school a generation ago. A sampling of these is sufficient to allow him to introduce, in a meaningful way, his own essays. His aim in these letters—beyond relaying family news and entertaining morsels for adolescent consumption—was to entice his student son into his web of scholarly interests; at the same time he sought to steer him away from the less benign webs in which young students are occasionally apt to get caught. His prevailing tone of humorous concern was struck at the close of his first letter: "Keep reading on your own! Nothing will help you more scholastically in the long run. And do please remember that you read other books last summer than the 007 James Bond series."

No sooner had my father received my schedule of classes at St. Paul's—where he had preceded me three decades earlier, as his father had him (ours is a repetitive family)—than he wrote to reassure me about its implications:

> I studied your schedule with the greatest interest and it didn't seem too bad! Saturday morning looked pretty filled up but perhaps you can do some of that homework before Friday night. Of course I really don't know how much homework they give you.

Every now and then I dream that I am back in school or college as a student, and despite my protests that I have *graduated* it never seems to make much impression. Sometimes it all seems much harder the second time around, as I am sure I would find it now. And in my dreams I never seem to be able to get my homework done—particularly when it comes to something really major like a senior thesis at college. They say that people who have nightmares like this really did very well and were conscientious when they were students. But do not let the prospect of future bad dreams discourage you! It's all part of the price you have to pay for making an extra effort, but it's really worth it, despite the ancient Greek motto: *mēden agan.*

(To my puzzled query, he subsequently supplied a free translation: "Don't overdo it.")

He had already persuaded me to sign up for ancient Greek, *in addition to Latin*, my first year at the school: his deep love of the classic languages is one of the golden threads of his web, as the reader will discover. My first Greek assignment—learning the alphabet—was tearful. But I soon recovered. He rushed to bolster my decision to stick with it: "I am glad that you do not find Greek quite as impossible as it seemed at first appearance. It is the most beautiful language and the things you will read in Greek were the models for the literature of later periods. You will *never* be sorry you took Greek, I promise you." By the end of the school year I was fully sold on Greek. But in picking courses for the next (fourth form) year I had planned to drop Latin—without his prior consultation—and this almost created an international crisis: "As for dropping Latin next year," he wrote,

> I think it is a good plan *if and only if* you will be picking it up again in your 5th form year. I really think it would be a mistake to have gone this far with Latin only to drop it now, and if I ever expected you to do that I never should have advised you to start

Greek. Please let me know if it was your understanding with Mr. Hall and Mr. Greaves to drop Latin only temporarily, that is, for the next year. If that is your plan I'll be glad to stay out of the discussion. Otherwise I really should like to find out more about the program you are mapping out. Needless to say I am very keen about Greek and again feel it would be a great mistake not to carry on with that, too. Also you should have a taste of a good science course before you get to college. But it would be very unwise for you to drop Latin for good at this point. Please write your father a reassuring letter about this or call him as he is most disconcerted!

Two weeks passed, in silence.

Not having heard any more about the schedule of courses for the 4th and 5th forms, I telephoned Mr. Hall to register my doubts as to the wisdom of dropping Latin for good at this point. As you will remember, you and I went up to St. Paul's to discuss these questions with Mr. Clark, and I really would never have ventured to get you to take up Greek if I had thought it would be at the price of dropping Latin. He agreed, and I am certain that Mr. Stuckey would agree with me about that, although possibly you could get away with skipping a year of Latin. I don't know about that. In any case I judge that you really do appreciate the fascination and beauty of the Greek language. The literature is probably the greatest treasure of our civilization and I know that you will always be grateful for getting to know it in its own tongue.

His prediction was on the mark: I was to continue reading Greek for the remaining three years of school and my first two years at Princeton, before being seduced for good by art history.

My father's letters reveal, as well, his love of classical music, which he pursued via the phonograph—his chosen instrument, I called it. He constantly wrote of new records he had purchased and was most supportive of my piano studies, which I had earlier intended to lead to a professional career. "I think you are wise not to bite off more than you can chew. After your studies, music is virtually an obligation in the light of the years you put into it and your own ability. You'll never really have an opportunity to *master* the piano later if you don't do so now. And once you have mastered it you'll be able to keep up a repertory all your life—adding new pieces from time to time." Once again, on the mark. Though my career was never to be at the keyboard, I still find myself there, after hours.

One of the Scribner authors my father worked closely with was the great South African novelist Alan Paton. I suppose it was a mixture of pride and pragmatism that prompted me to choose Paton's *Cry, the Beloved Country* as the subject of my first English term paper. My father wrote that he had sent my ideas about the novel to Paton, who was then under virtual house arrest in his native land, "as I felt sure that he would enjoy reading your reaction," he explained. (You may imagine the fourteen-year-old's delight.) "I believe that your book report will be a very good one, particularly if you include references to *Tales from a Troubled Land*. It might interest you to know that I thought up that particular title. It seemed to me that 'Troubled Land' made a nice echo of 'Beloved Country.'" A few weeks later he reported back on my paper—before I felt safe to submit it. Having declared that it "would pass in a college freshman course," he got down to basics: "One note to be careful about—your spelling falters occasionally. Be sure to check words like 'tragic' in the dictionary. Alan Paton told me that your typewriter must be a very old one since it spelled 'excellent' as 'excellant' and 'miracle' as 'miricle.' But he was very pleased by what you said about his book. I'll show you his letter."

My father's literary horizons extended well beyond Scribners' roster of authors. The summer before, he had assigned me a fifty-dollar reading list of English and American classics: I got paid on completion—a hefty sum for a jobless teenager in 1965! Once at school, I got a new list—the best books I've ever read—with an occasional comment from the professor: "I am delighted you liked the Chekhov stories. I was a sixth former at St. Paul's when I read these first and I still remember the impression they made on me. I thought they were beautifully written. There are so many other wonderful collections of short stories for you to become familiar with, e.g. Tolstoy, de Maupassant, Joyce, Hemingway, that I can't wait to have you start on the next $50 or $75 list! I am also anxious to read your own story." (It was, predictably, ersatz Chekhov, about a desperately lonely boy at a St. Petersburg prep school. Published in our school magazine, it panicked my housemaster until I reassured him that the story reflected only my *reading*, not my life.)

By my second year I had immersed myself in dramatics. My first major role, Cassius in Shakespeare's *Julius Caesar*, elicited a fatherly insight: "I reread *Julius Caesar* and was surprised to find Cassius a far more sympathetic character than I remembered him. I imagine the 'lean and hungry look' has struck and prejudiced readers. The introduction to your edition of the play was especially interesting in this respect since it showed how frustrated Cassius must have been to have every practical suggestion brushed aside by the starry-eyed Brutus! Did you find that difficult to convey?" In fact, I was mildly disturbed by how *easily* I identified with the cynical Cassius: I couldn't fault him. But now I wonder about my father's sympathy with Cassius's frustrated practicality. "Starry eyed" sons are equally prone to brushing off sound advice. Perhaps, I reluctantly conclude in hindsight, he was able to identify from paternal experience.

In any case, he proceeded to prescribe a program of study for a series of prize scholarship exams I was scheduled to take, with special emphasis on how to survive Caesar's *Gallic Wars*. I'll spare you these details (three single-spaced pages) worthy of the Roman general himself. But his campaign to capture the Shakespeare prize is worth quoting in full:

> I know all of this may be time consuming, but it could help you very much and there's nothing more nightmarish or frightening than to step into an exam unprepared. That was my own experience since I did absolutely no preparatory work at all and still remember the miserable experience of trying to answer questions on things I had completely forgotten. As a matter of fact I was too dumb to find out what we would be examined on and in those days no one took the initiative in briefing you beforehand. The boy who won did find out in advance and cleaned up! When it came to the Whipple Medal in Shakespeare (it was "Much Ado About Nothing" that year) I got tricky myself and adopted the following strategy which only took a day or so:
>
> 1) reading something about the play and Shakespeare's sources and models
> 2) reading the play itself three times to get the plot and structure and characters clearly in mind
> 3) memorizing about a dozen passages from various parts of the play—some as short as one line, some five or ten lines. By sprinkling these throughout my answers I was able to convey the impression that I knew the entire play by heart! How could I lose—especially since I compared the alternation of sad and happy sections of the play with the 3rd movement of Beethoven's Seventh Symphony! Naturally this particular plan may not be possible with the exams you will be taking but what I want to emphasize is the effectiveness of having a "strategy," so to speak. It gives you a marvelous feeling of confidence, too, which is half the battle.

I didn't win, but there is no question that I had the best coach available.

One of my stumbling blocks was solid geometry. Math and science are two primary passions—indeed, avocations—of my father, then as now. He wasted no time in trying to get me over the hurdle: "I wish I could help you on the geometry originals. As you point out, a lot of this is confidence and it is possible to defeat yourself if you become too anxious. Often there is some simple trick or clue to a solution. Sometimes it is seeing a familiar theorem in an unusual setting." After much about angles, arcs, diagrams, and hypotenuses, he dropped this pearl of wisdom:

> In other words, *do* something; even if what you start to do may not be exactly right, it may put you on the track of a solution. Be sure that all the data you have in the hypothesis are brought into play. If everything in the hypothesis isn't capitalized on it means you aren't focusing on the particular situation involved. They will almost never give you irrelevant data in the hypothesis. It might help you to work over a number of fairly difficult originals as a way of reviewing. Practice on them will build up your confidence and like the London *Times* crossword puzzles show you some of the tricky things that may arise! Hope I haven't confused you by all these suggestions. Usually the solution to an original is very simple and straightforward once you see the essential elements of the problem.

He later had second thoughts about my fascination with the London *Times* puzzles, to which I had become addicted with the aid of my English drama coach. (The *New York Times*'s is kid stuff; if you are feeling masochistic, try the English version.) "Please don't leave one of these puzzles around," began his note accompanying a small triumph. "I said to myself that I'd just fill in one word but a day later I'd done the whole thing. Very hard: 13 down I got by remembering a verse from Coleridge's 'Xanadu.' 9 across I read years ago by H. G. Wells. Etc. Etc. I hereby retire from the *Times* Crossword Puzzle!"

He must have quietly despaired when I told him that I really didn't believe for a moment Galileo's law of gravity (any fool knows that big heavy things fall faster than small light ones, right?), but for the sake of passing the physical science course I would *pretend* to accept that law. Besides, I was preoccupied with my upcoming performance as Shakespeare's cavalier King Richard II. Once more unto the breach, the father charged with pen in hand:

> Sorry you have so much trouble in accepting 16th-century science. Of course, when one deals with objects falling in an atmosphere they are all subject to resistance or forces of air friction and obviously a bullet falls faster than a feather. But the laws of uniform acceleration abstract from atmospheric conditions and assume a perfect vacuum. In a vacuum is there any reason to think that a cannonball (for example), which can be thought of as a kind of gluing together of tiny pellets, should fall faster than any one pellet composing it? In an atmosphere the forces act on the *surface* of a falling object and since the volume and therefore mass of an object varies with the *cube* of a linear dimension while its surface area varies with the *square*, the smaller an object is made the more it is responsive to air resistance. *That's why dust floats!* But your natural insincerity obviously enables you to take positions contrary to what you believe to be the case. A wonderful attribute for an actor and apparently useful in the study of physical science.

He later reinforced his concern with a book—Watson and Crick's *The Double Helix*—on the exciting adventure culminating in the discovery of the DNA molecule: "It will only take an hour or so. I want you to have a picture of the beautiful and imaginative side of science as well as the lively, amusing personalities of some of the great creative scientists. It is also filled with English lore!" (He knew *that* would hook me.) His "science gene" evidently skipped a generation. I was never at home in the lab. Once I hooked up my Bunsen burner hose to the water faucet and then panicked at the gush of "liquid gas" that shot up to the ceiling and threatened to extinguish us all— or so I feared. "Eh, Scribner, did you try to light it?" chuckled the teacher.

CHARLES SCRIBNER, JR.

As a Princeton freshman, I tried once again and took a course aptly nicknamed "Physics for Poets." Someone once said that taking physics at Princeton was like trying to take a drink from a fire hose. I was nonetheless inspired by the history of science as the history of progressively beautiful—that is, clearer, simpler, more "economic"—explanations of the confusing, cluttered natural world around us. Exams were another matter. I recall one question about gravity (once again!) in particular: "Why can dogs and cats jump three or four times their height whereas human athletes can at best jump their own height?" Pressed for time, I could only answer, "Dogs and cats are amazing animals." (Unlike her son, my paternal grandmother, a lifelong animal lover, considered it a fine answer.) Yet my appreciation of science as a *fine art* finally dawned. Years later it proved invaluable in solving a problem of art history involving the original configuration of a Rubens tapestry cycle. When asked by art students, "What was the most important art course you took?" I reply, "Physics." It was worth the struggle.

I trust that, by now, the next question—"Who was your most influential teacher?"—has already been answered. It has been said that not every teacher is a parent, but every parent is a teacher. I've had the best. I did not intend to share so much of my tutelage, but I cannot help hoping that those wise—and witty—words of the master will take root in the next generation. Grandchildren often listen better than children. My own sons would be wise to take their grandfather's book to heart. There are grounds for hope. Last term, my eleven-year-old son Charlie wrote a school paper entitled "My Grandfather's Influence," which I feel compelled to reprint in full:

> When I was younger, I would sometimes go to my grandparents' house for a visit. Sometimes, while my grandmother was out, my grandfather, who was deeply into science, would listen to science tapes for a very long time in his study. At the time, I was

more interested in television than most other things. Just to be nice, I would usually sit in the study with him and listen to the tapes. While drowning in my own boredom, as if the study was a torture room and the tapes were the torturers, I would hardly listen, and even if I did, I didn't try to understand at such a young age. One day, my grandfather started talking to me about it and I actually found it quite intriguing. I started to listen to the tapes with him as well as doing experiments. I became interested in Polywater, which was a fluke theory from the 70's by Russian scientists that said that the world water supply would be contaminated. My grandfather and I started to debate different ideas also. Now that I am older, I can relate to what is on the tapes more. Because of the many times talking to my grandfather, it has influenced my love of science greatly, making it one of my most favorite subjects, in and out of school.

I am reminded of that wonderful insight of Henry Adams, who wrote that a teacher may never know the extent of his influence. "A teacher," Adams concluded, "affects eternity."

Charles Scribner III

New York, October 1992

I

A Publisher's Progress

The Allure
of Great Books

☙

Growing up in a publishing family was inevitably a bookish experience; it prepared me to take over the family publishing business, although in ways derived from my other early loves that neither I nor my family could have foreseen. My father would almost always bring home galley proofs of new publications on which he would sometimes write corrections or alterations, using the stub of a very unsharpened pencil that he called an editorial pencil. Why editors do not use full-length pencils and why they do not sharpen them is a mystery I have never solved. These tools of the trade created in me the impression of a business world that was very primitive and set in its ways.

I should add that my first encounter with publishing was as an author. At the age of seven or eight I wrote a detective story, entitled *The Old Brick House of Mystery*. One of my grandfather's authors persuaded him to have it printed and bound— all eight pages of it. This was a useful experience of the trade from the writer's side.

My father would from time to time bring authors for a visit to our country home. That is how I came to know Marjorie Kinnan Rawlings and the great detective-story writer S. S. Van Dine (Willard Huntington Wright), among other less well-known Scribner writers. I never did meet Thomas Wolfe or F. Scott Fitzgerald, because I was away at boarding school, but they were close friends of my parents. Today, weekend visits by authors to their publishers' homes are less frequent. Most homes are smaller, and life moves at a faster pace.

Despite my growing up among literary lions, the reading that influenced me most deeply dated back almost two thousand years. As a boarding student at St. Paul's in Concord, New Hampshire, I was fortunately able to build on my earlier exposure to Latin. Though a good deal of the instruction left much to be desired, I had the good fortune to be invited in the fall of 1938 to sign up for a special class in Roman literature. We read selections from Livy, Plautus, Horace, and Catullus. The teacher, a man named Morris, truly loved these works, and his enthusiasm was contagious. Almost everything I learned that year has stuck in my mind.

When I entered Princeton in the fall of 1939, the university was enjoying something of a humanistic revival in the undergraduate curriculum, with various programs and courses introduced to provide a broader view of the arts. The recitations in the classics courses I took were not greatly different in structure from those of St. Paul's, but the content was incomparably richer. Princeton has a single faculty, and underclassmen have the great benefit of being taught by professors who also teach graduate students. I profited by this arrangement. The scholarship of these senior men enabled them to bring us close to the original meanings and associations of the masterpieces we were reading. And there were other advantages to this contact with eminent humanists. It was in a course in Horace that I was given an understanding of poetic technique that I have never had to revise. That was in a period when T. S. Eliot and the New Critics were pontificating on all aspects of literature, and I have always been grateful that classical studies provided me with other points of view. It was not unhelpful, for example, to know that Eliot's translation of Propertius fell far short of the mark.

The most rewarding decision I made at Princeton was to take up Greek. As I indicated above, for the purpose of mastering the language it was clearly too little and too late. Still, there were for me some lasting benefits, despite a volatile vocabulary and a feeble grasp of the grammar. It was a great thrill to read anything in Greek, and I still recall the first sentences of the Gospel of Saint John that began our study: "In the beginning was the Word"—most appropriate for the situation.

One required course in philosophy, as I remember, was pretty much devoted to the dialogues of Plato. The reason for this seemingly strange literary form as a medium for philosophy lies in the fact that for the Greeks the oral tradition was so powerful that even when they were reading to themselves they read out loud. Much of their science and other learning was conveyed by the spoken word in dialogues, lectures, and old-time bull sessions. The dialogue has other merits as well: it makes it possible to show a discussion among several speakers with conflicting views. It's fair to say that Socrates dominated in a sometimes irritating, know-it-all vein, but Plato got his point across on all the great issues that still occupy our minds. The writings of these ancient Greeks included those of Aristotle, who was a polymath—that is, he covered all fields, including logic, biology, literature, and ethics, to name just a few of the subjects he established. It seems that Aristotle used the spoken word in his teaching. Indeed, his method was called "peripatetic" because he walked up and down beside or among his students, a less formal way than that of our teachers today, who depend largely on a lectern and a blackboard. Oddly enough, we possess Aristotle's teachings today because one or another of his students took extensive notes. This core of ancient knowledge would prove useful later in my readings in the history of science.

At Princeton our teachers pushed us quite early into the translation of selections from the Greek masterpieces. After little more than a year of Greek, Professor Sam Atkins assigned us the translation of the first scene of Aeschylus's *Prometheus Bound*. In the following years we were reading Sophocles, Euripedes, Plato, and Homer. I remember the Ginn texts in green buckram of the plays, annotated by the English classicist Jebb. How I would love to have some of those volumes now.

After Pearl Harbor, when many undergraduates were accelerating their studies in order to enter the armed services, the classics continued to play a role in my life—an unexpected role. It was Francis Godolphin, also a Princeton classicist, who recruited me as a candidate for the cryptanalytic group in the U.S. Navy known as OP20-G. The team I was assigned to was responsible for the decipherment of the Japanese Naval Code JN 25. One colleague in OP20-G was a young Harvard classical scholar named John Moore. I remember his writing under a particularly difficult problem of decipherment an aphorism from the Greek Anthology: "Under every stone there is a scorpion." John wrote this in the original Greek. All told, I spent five years in cryptanalytic work. Despite its frustrations I enjoyed the work greatly. At school and college, when I had struggled to assemble the scattered words of a Horatian ode into a correct and coherent whole, I never thought that that task (which I still do not find easy) might lead to pinpointing the position of some ill-fated Japanese freighter in the middle of the Pacific Ocean. The Greeks had words for such ironies.

For me the classics have also been invaluable in studying and learning to appreciate stylistic elegance. Each word in Latin and Greek seems to have a solidity and weight that makes further modification superfluous. One senses the user's delight in the beauty of the language itself. As I said, in their writings the ancients were never far from the spoken word. Their poems, their plays, their history, and (if Aristotle is any clue) even their science seem to be composed for our ears rather than our eyes.

Even as a book publisher for the past forty-odd years I did not lose all contact with classical studies. Scribners was fortunate enough to have published Rolfe Humphries's translation of the *Aeneid*, and we have brought out a number of books on ancient history by Michael Grant, including the three-volume *Civilization of the Ancient Mediterranean: Greece and Rome* he coedited with Rachel Kittzinger of Vassar College. James Luce, chairman of the Classics Department at Princeton, also edited for us a two-volume set containing critical biographies of the ancient writers.

Another equally invaluable reading experience was my exposure at St. Paul's to an engaging series of books called the Modern Library. This series was founded in the 1920s by the New York firm of Boni and Liveright and was continued by Bennett Cerf at Random House. I am sure that virtually all the other book lovers of that period, many of them much older than myself, reveled in the variety and quality of that reprint series; it made an indelible mark on readers of all ages, but especially the young. I am glad to learn that after a lapse of some thirty years the Modern Library was relaunched in 1992 with much fanfare by Random House, in book form and also on computer disks.

The list of books that began the Modern Library shows that the editors had an uncanny knack for assembling titles—enticing by their authors and subjects—that were sure to appeal to anyone with a spark of intellectual curiosity and love of literature. I have tried to do the same with the "reading-reference books" issued by the Scribner Reference Department. It is clear, too, that the makers of the Modern Library managed to acquire for their imprint many of the great authors of the period, including Sherwood Anderson, Ernest Hemingway, F. Scott Fitzgerald, William Faulkner, John Steinbeck, and a galaxy of foreign writers of the first rank. For the authors it was a prestigious event to have their books selected by the series, which in turn made it difficult for the original publishers to refuse licensing them.

All kinds of books had been licensed to Boni and Liveright's successors while my father was alive. After his death in 1952, however, it became apparent that it would be very much to Hemingway's advantage if Scribners took the titles back from the Modern Library and published them itself. Many of the other great authors had a strong nostalgia, as well as gratitude, for the Modern Library, since some of their works had first won fame as a result of their presence in the series. When I wrote to Hemingway many years later that I was going to cancel the licenses to Bennett Cerf for his books, it was clear that although he could use the financial advantages, he winced a little at giving up a long-standing connection with the Modern Library, which had been such a source of pride during his early years.

Physically, the books were uniform in size, bound initially in fabrikoid and later in cloth and brandishing a little colophon that acted as a kind of seal of approval for so many of us. One of the titles that have become a part of my literary imagination is *Jurgen*, by James Branch Cabell. Considered slightly decadent (as well as indecent), the book made us young bloods think we were very smart and advanced to be reading it. At the same time, much of it was cryptic, and I'm not sure we had the slightest idea of what the author was talking about. No matter, we thought we were the absolute zenith of sophistication and picked up a great deal of its jargon.

Another Modern Library prize was *Precious Bane*, by Mary Webb, one of the most touching novels ever written, which was adapted for television not long ago and broadcast on Masterpiece Theatre. Other titles I remember with pleasure were *Heart of Darkness* and *Lord Jim*, by Joseph Conrad; *Sister Carrie*, by Theodore Dreiser; *Winesburg, Ohio*, by Sherwood Anderson; *Tortilla Flat* and *In Dubious Battle*, by John Steinbeck; *Short Stories*, by Anton Chekhov; *The Dance of Life*, by Havilock Ellis; *Sanctuary*, by William Faulkner; *Madame Bovary*, by Gustave Flaubert; *Thaïs*, by Anatole France; *The Great Gatsby*, by Fitzgerald; *The Apple Tree*, by John Galsworthy; *The Sorrows of Werther*, by Goethe; *Jude the Obscure*, by Thomas Hardy; *The Sun Also Rises* and *A Farewell to Arms*, by Hemingway; *Green Mansions*, by W. H. Hudson; *The Enormous Room* by e. e. cummings; *Point Counterpoint*, by Aldous Huxley; *The Turn of the Screw*, by Henry James; *The Philosophy of William James*, by James; and *Dubliners*, by James Joyce. It's still a good list!

Early on, I set myself the task of reading every book in the Modern Library, but I was somewhat daunted by Thomas Carlyle's *History of the French Revolution*. My intention threatened to break down at the thought of Carlyle, yet whenever I saw a "Modern Library" on display I couldn't resist buying it. I went on foraging trips to The Apple Tree Bookstore in Concord (which is still in business); to Bloomingdale's in New York, where they gave twenty feet or so of the mezzanine to the Modern Library, all in a horizontal line; and to the Princeton

University Bookstore, where a whole section was devoted to the series. I plundered them all, but I am afraid that I purchased more than I was able to read; I still possess some that I haven't read. They gaze at me reproachfully for my dereliction. Fortunately, it wasn't all selfish, for I created a lending library in my hometown of Far Hills, New Jersey. Some of my friends there still treasure their own collections of Modern Library books and experience the same enjoyment I do when they come across one of the early titles in a book barn or rummage sale. To turn around Louis Auchincloss's autobiographical maxim, "a publisher's capital is his reading."

Confessions of
a Book Publisher

&

I have been a book publisher almost all of my working life. Scribners has always been a family business, and when I joined the company in 1946 it was celebrating its hundredth anniversary.* At times I have been somewhat daunted by the weight of such a past, and I often think about how the three earlier generations of Scribners might view the present publishing scene.

Certainly they would have expected that the book business, like any other business, would change with the times. But I doubt whether in their wildest dreams they could have foreseen some of the developments that have taken place.

I wonder, too, how my great-grandfather Scribner would react to certain books that are now on the best-seller lists. His first publication in 1846 was a pious work entitled *The Puritans and Their Principles*. This gave an extremely sectarian version of church history, with no stone left unturned for the evil things

---

*See Appendices for a brief history of the company.

that might crawl out from under it. The author clearly had no use for bishops; he could see no place for them in the divine plan: certainly not on earth and probably not in heaven either. The chapter titles are revealing: "Episcopal Exclusiveness—Its Basic Superstition" or "Apostolical Succession, Corrupt as a Doctrine, False in Fact." You don't have to understand all the words to get the message.

It would be interesting to hear my great-grandfather's views on that modern classic *The Joy of Sex* or to have him compare the novels of Jane Austen with those of Erica Jong. In the words of Shelley, "the sense faints" imagining what he might say.

I really cannot speak for my Scribner forebears, but I can tell you that publishing is a strange business. At times it seems like stretching a point to call it a business at all. And yet we manufacture a product and sell it through wholesale outlets just like a record company, a television manufacturer, or even a producer of canned soups. In the most general definition, publishing firms are set up to provide authors with certain necessary services. We take an author's manuscript, edit it, and make it into a book. Then we try to make it available to the public as widely as possible through bookstores, libraries, and other channels. The author is paid for what he or she has written by receiving a certain portion of the money earned by the book.

It sounds very simple, doesn't it? Well, I can assure you that it is not simple in practice. At each stage of the operation, problems can crop up comparable to the difficulty of finding a cure for the common cold.

Sometimes a problem arises at the very beginning, for very often the author, or the literary agent representing the writer, does not come to you after the book has been completed, but before it has been begun. If an interesting idea for a book is submitted by a well-known author—someone with a proven ability to write and to stick with a commitment—there is no question about wanting to go ahead with it. The only trouble may be the amount of money you have to pay "up front" to close the deal. Many important and successful books have been commissioned in this way, including William Shirer's *Rise and Fall of the Third Reich*.

In an age where more and more books come from literary agents and the stakes are high in the bidding wars, one certainly yearns for the miracle of a Margaret Mitchell delivering to you, and you alone, the complete text of a *Gone With the Wind*. Some books do still come in out of the blue in that way. There are not many, but when they are published prosperously they add to the excitement of being a publisher. In the early 1970s an author named Clare Barroll came in to see me bringing with her the manuscript of a novel based on the lives of the Vikings. She and her husband had lived in Stockholm for many years while he was serving there as a representative for General Motors. During that period she studied the history of Scandinavia in the Middle Ages, and her book was based on extensive research. We published the novel under the title *The Iron Crown* and later brought out a very successful second book of hers entitled *Season of the Heart*.

I asked Mrs. Barroll how she happened to have brought her book to Scribners. It seems that as a little girl of nine or ten she had submitted a poem to *Scribner's Magazine*. That was in my grandfather's day. And recently she had heard me read the lesson during a Christmas service St. Bartholomew's Church in New York City. One reason why she submitted her novel to us was that she liked the way I read the Bible. This episode has given me a new sense of the importance of lay participation in church services. I have read the lesson devoutly several times since then, but no more such best-sellers have come our way.

For almost every writer the key individual in a publishing house is the editor who will guide the author through the process of turning a manuscript into a finished book. During those months, many authors are in a very sensitive condition, and their mood is likely to swing wildly between euphoria and gloom. So, in addition to all the technical skills that editors must provide, their moral support is needed too.

Some editors have become legendary for their ability to perceive genius in fledgling writers and for their patience and tact in handling literary prima donnas. Perhaps the most famous of those editors was Maxwell Perkins at Scribners. Perkins is an important figure in American literature because of the support and encouragement he gave to almost a whole generation of young American writers, beginning in the twenties. Perhaps his most impressive single accomplishment as an editor was to carve two best-selling novels by Thomas Wolfe out of what must have been close to a ton of raw manuscript.

Perkins was also the editor and friend of Ernest Hemingway, and while Hemingway did not need the kind of help that Wolfe did, he sometimes expected special services. One year, he left his fly-fishing rods in safekeeping with Perkins. Somehow or other the tip of one of the rods got broken and there was an uproar about that. Scribners was blamed for criminal negligence and almost lost its most celebrated author. At that time we were also faithfully storing cartons of Hemingway's shotgun shells in the plate vaults of our printing plant on Forty-third Street. Had the building blown up we would undoubtedly have been blamed for that also.

Nowadays, when young people come looking for jobs with Scribners, they usually profess willingness to start work in any part of the business. But we know that in their heart of hearts almost all of them want to become editors—and the sooner the better. The glamour of the title "book editor" has great appeal.

Little do they know about the anxieties arising from fishing tackle and ammunition.

You might suppose that printing and binding the books would be a comparatively uneventful part of publishing. Nothing could be further from the truth. Many years ago, in the time of Johannes Gutenberg, the Devil was alarmed by the sudden proliferation of Holy Bibles. So he assigned an army of gremlins to monitor printing plants. It was their mission to make sure that from then on as many things as possible would go wrong. That army was superbly trained and, believe me, it is still on the job. At times it has made me wish that I were in a less vulnerable business—something practically foolproof, like producing canned vichyssoise.

One memorable experience with the Devil's crew occurred in the mid 1970s when Scribners was publishing a beautiful engagement calendar for the Sierra Club. It was illustrated in four colors, and we were printing it in hundreds of thousands of copies. It was one of our most massive publications. To separate the "work week" from the weekend, we had decided to start the page for each week with Monday instead of Sunday (that in itself ought to have placated the Devil). But in making the necessary changes someone blundered, and two weeks in July were printed with incorrect dates—Monday was given the date for Tuesday, Tuesday the one for Wednesday, and so on for two pages. It was an awesome catastrophe.

How could we face the prospect of all that might go wrong in the lives of our trusting customers during those two weeks? We imagined all the airline flights missed and displaced anniversaries, the marriages without bridegrooms, and the surgical operations without patients. It was unthinkable just to sit back and hope for the best. So we set to work and corrected every one of those calendars by hand. It took us weeks and cost us a fortune. But it had to be done.

That was the biggest hand-to-hand encounter with the Devil. I cannot say that we routed his army, but we won the battle and saved the day. In fact we saved fourteen days. Yet as far as I can see now there is not the slightest prospect of a truce.

Over the years I have learned many interesting things about our business by going through the daily orders. Doing that is also very good for the morale, since you can almost hear the cash register ringing in the background. My pleasure in seeing an order is usually in proportion to its size, but I occasionally find some that are delightful for other reasons.

For example, in 1948 we published a collection of sermons by Paul Tillich. It was brought out under the title *The Shaking of the Foundations*, and I remember the morning when I saw the order for one copy of the book, which came from a construction company. Another time I noticed that a certain bank was sending us an annual order for several hundred copies of a book called *You and Psychiatry*. We knew that banks had all kinds of problems, but it was hard to believe that one bank could have so many psychiatric ones. The puzzle was never cleared up. My prize discovery was an order from the U.S. Army Signal Corps in Pennsville, New Jersey, for a single copy of *The Boy's First Book of Radio and Electronics*. Was this purchase charged to the defense budget? It was an alarming thought, which returned to me during the war years that followed.

Publishing books has been one of the most fascinating occupations I can imagine. At the same time it is also one of the most frustrating. It is fascinating because you are continually dealing in ideas—some of them so fresh and so daring that they will perhaps turn into forces that change the world. You are also dealing with the men and women who create these ideas and exert themselves to bring them to life in the minds of their readers. Without great writers and their original ideas, our world would be something like a phonograph record that keeps going round and round—endlessly repeating the same tune or fragment of a tune. A great writer lifts up the arm of the record player and sets the needle down in a new groove. Every generation needs men and women who can perform that feat for their contemporaries, and so far every generation has been fortunate in having its share of such writers.

The most rewarding part of my job has been the privilege of knowing hundreds of authors. They are sensitive, intelligent, delightful men and women. All the life that flows through their books stems directly and naturally from their total interest, their passionate engagement in the world around them.

I am sorry I was not old enough to know Scott Fitzgerald, that tormented, courageous man whose books are more successful now than at any time during his life. Scott could never have imagined how many millions of *The Great Gatsby* would be sold after his death. He would never have supposed that it would eventually replace *Silas Marner* as the standard novel for high school students.

I also regret not becoming acquainted with Thomas Wolfe. He was so tall that he used to write his books on the lid of an icebox instead of at a desk, and Wolfe used to sleep on the floor of Scribners' library during the months he was trying to read every book we had ever published.

Ernest Hemingway and I worked together in the decade between my father's death in 1952 and his in 1961. He was a tremendously loyal man. I was in the navy when my father died. Hemingway and I had never met, but he wrote to me in Washington to say that I would never have to worry about his loyalty to Scribners. One day he visited me in my office, and after I went out to get him a cup of coffee I came back to find him sitting at my desk. He was only trying to be informal and put me at my ease. He had no idea what a profoundly demoralizing, emasculating experience it is for a businessman to have to sit in front of his own desk. It took me days to recover.

I also treasure my friendship with Alan Paton, who in 1947 sent his beautiful novel *Cry, the Beloved Country* to Scribners to publish, a book that has had worldwide impact, notably on the reform movement in his native South Africa. Alan could be dour at times, and he was also an incorrigible tease. When he visited us he liked to bait me and show up my ignorance, asking me all kinds of questions about everything he saw in America, such as the names of all the trees we happened to pass on the New Jersey Turnpike. Occasionally, I had the temerity to quote Shakespeare to Alan, at which times he delighted in telling me that my American accent was so bad he couldn't understand a word. And so it went.

Another great friend of ours was C. P. Snow, later "his lordship." Possibly no foreigner ever received as many American honorary degrees as he did after his view of "the two cultures"—science and the humanities—swept the world. Charles was an extremely shrewd judge of character and this ability lay at the very center of his fiction. Among my intellectual debts to him, not the least was his persuading me to read Anthony Trollope.

To many admirers of Snow he embodied scientific objectivity and cool professionalism. But I saw in him a man who had been born into a humble middle-class family and raised himself to a high place by dint of a keen mind and an iron determination. In later life he was able to move in what he called the corridors of power, but the boy inside him could never quite believe what had happened and could never wholly shake off his romantic fascination with people in high places. That boy was the source of his charm.

He happened to be in New York in 1969, when the Mets were winning the National League pennant and later the World Series. Although he had thought his heart belonged to cricket, he fell head over heels in love with baseball. Like the rest of us he ended up glued to a television set. He even asked Burroughs Mitchell, his editor at Scribners, to buy him a regulation baseball, and one day, when Burroughs came to visit Lord Snow in his suite at the Westbury Hotel, he found the great man sitting in an armchair throwing the baseball into a sofa.

I said that I found book publishing frustrating as well as fascinating. Living and working with books as I have, I find that reading them professionally or for pleasure has left me with a little knowledge about almost every subject but not a great deal about any. Let me give you some idea of how haphazard my reading really has been. In the course of one month in the mid 1970s I had to read the following books, mostly in manuscript. First, a novel about Christopher Columbus. According to the author, Columbus had actually sailed to North America on a Norwegian boat and spent some time in the New World many years before his famous voyage of 1492. That is why he was so certain that his official voyage would be a success. Next, about the same time, I perused a book that explained how various creatures such as birds, eels, and salmon navigate and find their way about the earth (a subject perhaps not wholly unrelated to Columbus's voyages). Then I had to go through a book that explained how the fossil bones of dinosaurs and other extinct animals are dug up and put back together by paleontologists. After that sobering vision, I was digesting a book that outlined how some of the giant American corporations failed to make a go of it in Europe after World War II. In the same month, I enjoyed the biography of the woman novelist and poet Radclyffe Hall, whose novel *The Well of Loneliness* shocked readers in the twenties. I savored the memoirs of an American woman reporter in World War II, a spy-thriller set in present-day Egypt and Cyprus, plus a science fiction story about implanting a human brain in the skull of a whale (the whale committed suicide). I also worked through a scholarly study about the kinds of people who made up the audiences when Shakespeare's plays were being performed for the first time. This was followed by a report on the scientific work of the German physicist Max Planck and the life story of an English spastic who had spent his life in a hospital, barely able to move or speak. Last but by no means least I examined with care the plan for an encyclopedia of the Middle Ages and a critical dictionary of English writers.

As you can imagine, my mind was often reeling after reading such a jumble of topics. I used to try to restore my equilibrium by reading the novels of Anthony Trollope in the evenings. The net result of reading books in so many different fields, month after month, year after year, is that my mind has become something like an automobile junkyard. You can find spare parts for almost any kind of car, but you won't find a single car you can drive.

A different kind of discomfiture overtakes a publisher when he feels in his bones that he has discovered a great new writer, only to find that for some mysterious reason he or she is neglected by the critics and the reading public. This often happens at a time when essentially shallow books by essentially shallow writers are climbing to the top of the best-seller lists. Such a deep disappointment has always made me worry and ask myself where I may have failed in my effort to promote that book so that it would reach the public.

Let me mention two examples of this concern. The first was a novel about a Florida chain gang by a writer named Donn Pierce. I read it in manuscript and felt convinced it should be a winner; it had some of the magic of Steinbeck's *Of Mice and Men*. As it turned out, it sold disappointingly in book form but later, in 1967, became the very successful motion picture *Cool Hand Luke*, starring Paul Newman. It wasn't just Newman's doing, either: it was a great story. The second book was a Civil War novel, *The Falling Hills*, by a dazzlingly gifted young writer named Perry Lentz. This book sold very well for a first novel—close to 10,000 copies. But I think that with better luck it might have been a famous best-seller.

Another frustrating thing is that almost everyone—the man in the street, members of your own family, members of every author's family, and numberless strangers—professes to know a great deal more about book publishing than you do. Sometimes I tell myself that even if I were the village idiot I would inevitably have learned more about the book business in forty-six years of practice than someone who has never been in it a day. But it's a losing battle.

The first time I encountered this sort of omniscience on the part of the outsider was shortly after I had got out of the navy and was working in Scribners advertising department. A man called me up from one of the movie studios in Hollywood. I remember waiting a long time after I got on the phone before his minion did put him on. He told me he was calling to ask the title of the last S. S. Van Dine mystery we had published. When I gave him the title it seemed to annoy him. "But that was five years ago. Haven't you published a Philo Vance mystery since then?"

"No," I said. "It so happened that after this last one the author died."

That annoyed my Hollywood friend even more. "Good Lord!" he exclaimed. "You didn't have to let the series die, did you?"

For more than one reason I avoid discussing the subject of publishing with people I do not know. If you tell a stranger that you publish books, various kinds of embarrassment may ensue. I may be asked to name some of our exciting new books. That particular question invariably plunges me into temporary amnesia; I find it hard to remember the title or author of *any* book that we have published recently. Nothing strange about that: a publisher is thinking most of the time about books still in production; on the spur of the moment he cannot be sure whether a given book has actually been *published* as yet. "Finished books" are in being some six weeks before "pub date," to give reviewers time to read and write their piece. But these and other details do not make it any less embarrassing to be stumped by innocent questions.

One is often put on the spot by a query one would rather not answer but cannot ignore. It usually involves a friend or relative of the person one is talking to. For example, would Scribners be interested in publishing a book of poems by a talented college freshman? His English professor thinks they are very unusual. As a matter of fact, we would almost certainly not be interested in publishing such a book, or in receiving the manuscript in the mail, return postage enclosed. In these situations you have to cultivate almost supernatural insincerity to make your answer sound kindly and instructive.

I am often asked whether Scribners published a particular book. Nine times out of ten we did not. If the book is a sensational best-seller, like Alex Haley's *Roots* or Leon Uris's *Trinity*, or has just been sold to a paperback reprinter for a million dollars, it is rather depressing to have to say no. If it is a very successful book we happened to have turned down, it is extremely depressing even to think about it. In either case it is not easy to make one's reply sound genuinely cheerful.

My grandfather missed one such golden opportunity to publish an enormously successful work when Bruce Barton of advertising giant BBD&O fame submitted to Scribners his version of the Gospel story. As our editor Maxwell Perkins explained it to my grandfather, the book portrayed Jesus as a super-salesman. Indeed, at that point this was the tentative title. My grandfather groaned in pain at the very idea of such a book, and he agreed that it should be declined then and there. Subsequently, the book was published in 1925 by another firm under the title *The Man Nobody Knows* and became one of the great best-sellers of the twenties. Of course, Mr. Perkins was called up on the carpet to explain why he had let such a successful book slip through his fingers. "But I told you it would sell," he said to my grandfather. "You didn't tell me it would sell 400,000 copies," my grandfather replied. They say he smiled when he said that, but I doubt it.

During my father's reign at Scribners, dealing with Winston Churchill proved a disappointing failure. Charles Scribner's Sons was Churchill's American publisher for several of his earliest books including *The River War*, *My Early Life: A Roving Commission* (which was a huge success), and his great work on World War I *The World Crisis*. With his proceeds from *The World Crisis*, Churchill purchased his country home. Later, Scribners entered into a contract with him for the biography of his great ancestor the duke of Marlborough. The multivolume set was called *Marlborough: His Life and Times*. Despite its prestige, this book turned out a financial failure; it was extremely expensive to produce and had virtually no popular success. Years later, when Masterpiece Theatre aired a television series on the first Churchills, I nursed a hope that a reissue of the set in paperback would pay its way, but its sales were disappointing.

My father had many social and business contacts with Churchill in both England and America. The man had a proclivity to what Hemingway called "joking rough." He never shied away from a joke or wisecrack that might be embarrassing to someone else. Powerful men often feel that they are above the squeamishness of others. Yet he showed surprising prudishness in another context. On one of his visits to New York in the 1930s he was hit by a taxicab when crossing the street after looking on the wrong side. While he was recuperating at Lenox Hill Hospital from this very serious accident, my father thought it might amuse the patient to read a bawdy (though by today's standards tame) humor magazine called *Bally-hoo*. It couldn't have been a worse choice. Churchill was outraged by the contents—his unexpected anger left my father somewhat stunned.

After World War II, Churchill's memoirs were obviously the greatest potential plum for a publisher. For a brief time my father may have hoped that Scribners would publish them. But as it turned out, the memoirs had already been acquired by Houghton Mifflin in concert with Time-Life. My father had paid a courtesy call on Churchill to see if he would let Scribners publish these memoirs. Churchill received him graciously and was sensible of the disappointment he was causing, but the deal for the book had already been made. Churchill was in bed resting. He started to get up, but my father, wanting to prevent needless exertion, restrained him from doing so by putting a hand on his shoulder. In that gesture he expressed his admiration and affection, while also letting Churchill know that he understood and respected his decision. Later, however, my father had misgivings about his spontaneous gesture: Had he gone too far in pushing the great man back?

I have been told that failures can be highly instructive. In the 1960s one of my colleagues at Scribners, Elinor Parker, and I went to see the people at Vogue-Butterick, the company that makes and sells dress patterns. We were trying to get their experts to write a new sewing book for Scribners. They did write the book, but they didn't write it for Scribners. *C'est la guerre!* But what was the lesson for us?

At one point in our tour of the Vogue-Butterick offices they took us into a little room in which the walls were covered with the illustrated envelopes, printed in full color, for all the dress patterns they had brought out during the last twelve months. They called this their "brain room." All these patterns tacked up on the wall were divided into twelve groups—one for each month of the year—and within each group the patterns were arranged in three subgroups: a small subgroup at the top, a large one in the middle, and another small one at the bottom. The top folders contained their most successful patterns for that particular month, the middle group comprised their average sellers, and the patterns at the bottom were their flops. Our hosts told us that they spent a lot of time in their "brain room" studying the different patterns and trying to figure out what made some popular and others not. They added that they thought they could learn more from their failures than from their successes. You could eventually discover the reasons for the failures, but the reasons for the spectacular successes usually remained a mystery.

That was reassuring to me, in two ways. First, I had never thought that we had a large enough number of best-sellers to conduct a scientific survey of them, and, second, I knew that we always had a sufficient number of books that did not sell very well. So perhaps now, at last, we were going to be in a position to learn something really solid; we might not be able to predict success, but we might discover the anatomy of failure.

Many years ago at a publishing conference I was talking with John O'Connor, at that time president of Grosset and Dunlap and an elder statesman in book publishing. I happened to speak a little disparagingly about a fellow publisher, accusing him of publishing on what I called an ad hoc basis. I meant by this that the publisher in question had no overall program but was simply taking on new books on a catch-as-catch-can basis. And being young and much more opinionated than I am now, I was quick to find fault with someone else's approach to the business.

O'Connor put me in my place. He said, "Charlie, publishing *is* an ad hoc business. That's the way you have to look at it." I've thought about John's statement several hundred times since then, and I must admit that it has been an important element in my publishing education. One must keep an open mind about the books one considers, and one must remain receptive to new possibilities on an ad hoc basis. But that does not mean that one may not have ideas and plans of one's own. Every publisher has his or her own dream list of books to publish if someone would only write them. That hope too is a crucial part of the business as well as an important part of the pleasure of publishing.

Louis Pasteur once said that in science "chance favors the prepared mind." That's another way of saying that you are more apt to see something if you're on the lookout for it. I think highly of that maxim, which has proven especially apt in describing the evolution of our reference department. At the beginning of the Korean War, I was called back to Washington for active duty in the navy. On the face of it this was a serious setback in my publishing career, since it cost me two years just at the time I was trying to learn the business. But in another way it was the most beneficial thing that could have happened to me. Since I was working on an eight to four schedule with no possibility of taking my work home (it was classified), I had the whole evening and weekends to read and study what I pleased—a luxury not afforded editors or publishers.

During this period I happened to subscribe to two scholarly journals: *Isis*, a journal devoted to the history of science, and the *Journal of the History of Ideas*. Reading these out of pure intellectual curiosity laid a foundation of knowledge that was enormously helpful when it came to expanding our reference book list; it resulted in our publishing the *Dictionary of the History of Ideas* (five volumes) and the *Dictionary of Scientific Biography* (sixteen volumes).

The success of these sets led us to initiate a program of reference works in virtually all areas of the humanities, American studies, intellectual history, world literature, world history, and the arts. Scribners has carried out perhaps the largest humanistic reference program ever undertaken. Right now the acorn of an early idea seems to have produced a still-growing oak tree of many branches. To change the metaphor, I sometimes think of reference-book publishing as planting a forsythia bush. The branches put down roots and the roots put up branches. It's hard to keep up with the process. I believe that similar possibilities of bringing out valuable works of instruction and intellectual pleasure lie all about us in their bush or acorn stage.

John O'Connor did teach me one great lesson about publishing, but my education in the field has been enlarged by other lessons acquired through trial and error. One of these has been how to detect a winning book from the sea of manuscripts that flows incessantly into a publisher's office. Every publisher who acts as reader and editor must surrender personally to a new novel just as the average reader does. Preconceived ideas of what a novel should be must be set aside in addition to any prejudices as to what the public will or won't like. The author must be allowed to engage the reader's interest in the most direct and simple way. If the publisher finds it hard to stop reading a manuscript, to stop turning the page, that's a good sign. If the publisher has brought half the work home to read over the weekend and ends up regretting not bringing the whole thing, that too is a wonderful sign, worth more than a dozen market surveys.

In general, the publisher comes to rely more and more on the effect a book has on him or her personally while reading it. This is a subjective test, but it's the safest in the long run. The best editors, like the best readers, really love books. They have the capacity to enjoy them, and they know how to put themselves in the author's hands in the way that is indispensable if the book is to come to life.

A book's "coming to life" is obviously *the* crucial test of every work of fiction. When it happens, the reader no longer feels that he or she is reading a book: the characters have become real people, and what happens in the story has the impact of actual experience. That's the reason a great book is an important cultural force. Great books create an enduring common experience shared by their readers all over the world. Eventually, the names of fictional characters become part of our vocabulary: Don Quixote, Scrooge, Sherlock Holmes, Dr. Jekyll, Mr. Hyde, Gatsby, Candide, Captain Queeg.

To produce an illusion of life in this way, writers give you little details about a character that will trigger your imagination and evoke a flesh-and-blood person: Oliver Twist asking for "more," Proust's narrator remembering the crumbs in the teacup, Sherlock Holmes filling his pipe out of the slipper on the mantelpiece, Tom Sawyer farming out the painting of the fence, Captain Queeg rattling the ballbearings in the palm of his hand. The more imaginative and effective these details, the less aware the reader is of the painstaking efforts that called them forth. To convey a genuine sense of life in a book is the hardest kind of work.

In publishing one also learns never to form an opinion about a book one has not read. I remember with anguish my browbeating our children's book editor into turning down a book that she described as a literary classic. My only reason for coercing her was the fact that it was about rabbits. If I had had the good sense—the common sense—to read a chapter or so, it is almost certain that I would have realized its merit. After we turned it down it was published by Macmillan with great success. The book was *Watership Down*, by Richard Adams.

When we published Alan Paton's *Cry, the Beloved Country* in 1948, some of my colleagues at Scribners tended to think of it as another of Max Perkins's kind-hearted gambles on an unknown writer. Even the judges at the Book-of-the-Month Club would not read it at first, despite a glowing review by one of their editors, John Barkham. Now, almost a half-century later, Paton's book is still one of our best-sellers every year. I need hardly say that experiences of this kind have given me a strong aversion to snap judgment.

Perhaps the most important lesson I learned was not to live in the past. This may sound like an unnecessary maxim for a professional who obviously has to keep up with the times, but one can be influenced and sometimes dominated by the past in imperceptible ways. In the early 1950s, when I succeeded my father as president of Scribners, the editorial achievements of Maxwell Perkins were still fresh in the minds of most of us. Since Perkins had been primarily interested in fiction, our editors had come to view that genre as being all-important. The result of this emphasis was that our list had become top-heavy in first novels, while our search for new books in the various categories of nonfiction—history, science, criticism, and practical arts—lagged behind.

The competition for new fiction having become so intense in the book industry generally, there came to be a gradual lowering of standards. The merest promise of talent was treated as tantamount to talent itself. This meant the weakening of our fiction list—of everyone's list—with the consequence that we all spent an exorbitant amount of time and money on novels that never made the grade. In his era Perkins himself would have been no more successful, for the times have changed. It took us years to realize the truth and to pursue other kinds of books more vigorously.

Today the book business is in a curious situation and it is difficult to guess what the future holds in store. I feel very uncertain about it. When I see what I would call the Hollywood-ization of contemporary publishing I am dismayed. But what disturbs me even more is the increasing tendency to regard books only as items of entertainment. The best-seller list has never been an accurate indicator of the books of enduring value produced in a given period, but as one looks at the best-selling titles of current years one gets the impression that the majority consists of ephemeral fiction and books cobbled together quickly about recent scandals, crimes, and fanatical causes on the one hand and vulgarized self-help manuals on the other. Many of these works have been promoted with all the fanfare and hype of contemporary public relations: special appearances of the author on TV; informal visits by reporters to the author's home, where reels of candid photographs are taken to illustrate a magazine article; continual releases of sales figures and details of big deals already made or in the offing— all these and other fan-magazine routines invented in Hollywood do not enhance the reputation of publishing as something better than mass production for mass taste.

In a curious way, some of these promotional techniques have come to infect the modern biographer when his subject is a writer. Someone researching the career of an author published by Scribners will invariably ask us to furnish the number of copies sold of his or her works, the size of the first printing, and royalty accounting questions more appropriate if they had come from a tax examiner.

Yet counterbalancing all the ballyhoo that accompanies blockbusters are many enlightened institutions that vigorously support serious works. Our academic and public libraries regularly buy new books—genuine books—in a wide variety of fields. To get a true view of the breadth of their interests one need only study the book notices in *Choice* or the *Library Journal*. There are also a number of specialized book clubs that advertise and distribute new books in their field—from science to military history. I am also an admirer of the service rendered to serious readers by general book clubs such as the Book-of-the-Month Club. All these clubs enable readers who lack a local bookstore to order books conveniently by mail; and more important still, clubs make it possible for those readers to know what books have just come out and what they are about.

It is also fitting to recall here the debt of gratitude that the book-publishing industry owes to the hundreds of newspapers and magazines throughout the country that regularly review new books. Few of these periodicals—let me add—get much recompense for this service in the form of book advertising, not even at Christmastime.

Of course, when one is describing the sources and fate of books today, the output of the university presses is of enormous importance. These publishers of scholarly works are responsible for a number of major projects such as the Jefferson Papers and other collected writings of great statesmen and scientists. I have served on the editorial board of the Einstein Papers, which are being published by Princeton University Press, and it is an inspiration to see the pains that are taken in making such a project as useful as possible for scholars. When people speak of the imminent demise of the book can they be aware of such undertakings? It is difficult to imagine that such a publication could have the same scholarly or educational value if it were available only as disks to be scanned in a data base, instead of being available, readable, consultable in book form.

University presses have also played a noble role in supporting the indigent muses of poetry. Many volumes of the work of certain poets are published under these rather unexpected auspices. And a further, late development—unless we go back to William Blake's self-illustrated poems—is the publication and distribution of certain highly specialized books by mail from the authors' own homes. It is unlikely that such sales are included in surveys of the industry.

Success in that mode of marketing reminds us that the greatest difficulties in publishing arise from the character and practices of bookstores. The chief difficulty is the so-called return privilege, by which unsold copies of a book are sent back to the publisher for credit. Given the bookstore's small space and high rental, the owner has no choice but to return the books. This has the devastating effect of reducing to a few months the exposure of a new book to its potential readers. After their return the books generally become unavailable—remaindered or otherwise hard to track down. This state of affairs is very costly and harmful to all parties involved—authors, publishers, booksellers, and readers. Some rational reform ought not to be beyond the wit of man to devise.

Additionally, the enormous popularity of paperback editions of current books has created a serious pricing problem for hardcover books in a period of accelerating inflation. The sales of all but the most successful hardcover titles have not expanded beyond the sales figures of the 1940s, and the falling off of the government support of libraries has worsened the situation yet further.

The upshot of these financial pressures is the frantic search for big books and the auctioning of obviously "hot" titles at unprecedented prices. The smaller or medium-sized firms that cannot afford to play for the highest stakes will inevitably have to reappraise their fundamental publishing objectives. In many cases this will lead to specialized publishing programs analogous to what Scribners has developed in the field of reference books. It will no longer be possible for a publisher to expect that various kinds of profitable books will come their way automatically.

Thomas Jefferson's biographer Dumas Malone once told me Jefferson's comment that man was a "bad weather animal." That is probably true of publishers. When the going gets rough one must try harder. One learns to be more resourceful. I believe that in the end the public will benefit from the greater difficulties that publishers face at this time. For one thing, there may be fewer books published. And those that are may be written and edited with more care.

The Secret of Being Ernest
(and the Secret of
Keeping Ernest)

❧

I t was seven decades ago that Ernest Hemingway met with
the famous Scribner editor Maxwell Perkins in the company's offices on Fifth Avenue. It was a fateful meeting, as it
led Hemingway to become a Scribner author, an association
that he maintained for the rest of his life. After his death in
1961, his widow, Mary, continued that loyalty to Scribners, and
with her cooperation we published ten of his works posthumously. In the 1980s we published a major novel, *The Garden
of Eden*, and brought out a final collection of his short stories. I
sincerely hope that if Ernest is keeping a watch on the fate of
his writings from someplace beyond the grave he will be
pleased by what we have done and what we are doing. If he is
not pleased I am sure to hear about it should we meet in the
hereafter.

Since Hemingway first cast his lot with our company his reputation has grown steadily to that of a world master. In the
course of his association with Scribners, three generations of
the family served as heads of the company, beginning with my
grandfather, who was a son of the founder. My father followed

in 1931, and I succeeded him twenty years later. That's a good many Scribners for one author to put up with, but Hemingway took us in stride. There was also a succession of editors who worked with Hemingway during the same period. The relationship with Scribners covered virtually his entire career as a writer.

Many of the details of that association are probably familiar to students of Hemingway's life and work. Given all that has been published about him, it could hardly be otherwise. Although I wrote in my 1990 book, *In the Company of Writers*, about my business relationship with Hemingway, I should like to take this opportunity to describe the private Hemingway as exhibited in his writings and personality. If my recollections convey the kindness and loyalty of that extraordinary man, I shall have achieved my purpose.

Thomas Wolfe (another Perkins author) set down the axiom "You can't go home again." Hemingway seems never to have made the attempt. Once he left Oak Park, Illinois, he left it for good. But leaving one's hometown is not that simple a thing. He left Oak Park, but Oak Park did not leave him. He carried it around in his head. I would venture to suggest that not a day of his life passed without some memory of a scene or event of his youth entering his stream of consciousness. Hemingway was born into a family of comfortable means, one in which there was sincere respect for the arts and the life of the mind. His mother, Grace, was a musician of professional competence, and his father, Clarence, a medical doctor, had the respect for knowledge and seriousness of purpose that went with his profession. Dr. Hemingway was also an experienced woodsman, an amateur naturalist, and a crack shot.

The influence of these interests on his son is unmistakable. I find it poignant to note that during a safari in Africa close to the end of his life Hemingway confessed that he wished he had learned more about birds.

In the Hemingway home Ernest absorbed a moral code virtually with his mother's milk. It comprised the conventional dos and don'ts of that time and that place, and like most such codes it was probably not thought about very much and certainly not revised. It was kept sacrosanct.

As a young man, Hemingway soon rebelled against conventional ethics, but he obviously continued to believe that a code of conduct was essential for life. Indeed, he went on to elaborate his own code in which he attached considerable importance to courage, memorably defined by him as grace under pressure. Like Chekhov he was more interested in the inner rather than the outer side of morality. What counted was what one was prepared to sacrifice for one's convictions, rather than what one gained by them. These moral concerns were an important part of his literary imagination; they inspired some of his finest stories and novels, from his early tale "Indian Camp" to his unfinished and posthumously published novel *The Garden of Eden*.

At the proper age, Hemingway was enrolled in the Oak Park and River Forest High School. What a splendid place that must have been! From the outside it had the venerable elegance of Nassau Hall at Princeton, which for some of us is the highest praise. But the school was equally marvelous inside. Those were the good old days of College Board essay examinations, before the numbing oppression of multiple-choice tests. In keeping with the humanistic curriculum, the school boasted a Latin Room, with Roman chairs and a stone desk, intended to create an appropriate atmosphere for studying Caesar, Cicero, and Virgil. There was also an Oxford Room with stained-glass windows and an enormous fireplace. For extracurricular activities the school had a theater in which students put on plays.

The school also sponsored a weekly newspaper, *The Trapeze*, and a literary magazine, *The Tabula*. Hemingway contributed to both. All writers enjoy seeing their work in print, but for Hemingway the pleasure became an addiction. Words came easily to him, and he had an inborn sense of style. He was, moreover, always on the lookout for material to shape into a story; he was a magpie in that respect, industriously and, almost by reflex action, storing away in his memory colorful bits and pieces of life.

I think that from the start there was a kind of enchantment about his commitment to writing. Robert Louis Stevenson, in his autobiographical essay "The Lantern-Bearers," describes the excitement he felt as a boy when he and his comrades would meet after dark, each carrying a bull's-eye lantern under his topcoat. All the lanterns were lit but kept covered for the greater part of the expedition. Only at the end were they uncovered and allowed to shine out full strength. Stevenson makes the point that for those boys roaming the streets of Edinburgh, the bliss in the adventure lay in the knowledge that the lanterns were illuminated and burning brightly even in the dark under their topcoats.

Like all true artists, Hemingway kept his own lantern under his topcoat, hidden from outsiders; he would talk about it tangentially, if at all. But it was there all the time, the most important thing in his life. His classmates recognized his talent and referred to him as "our Ring Lardner," the highest compliment they could pay him, and at that time by no means inappropriate.

The idea of becoming a professional writer was shaping itself in his mind. It was becoming such a powerful ambition that when the time came for him to think about college it could have been no great surprise to anyone that he chose instead a job as cub reporter on the Kansas City *Star*. He knew he had a bent for journalism, and the job was in line with his ambition.

Hemingway's six-month stint on the *Star* has been rightly described as an apprenticeship. He learned how to dig out the facts of a story, and he toiled at describing them simply and directly. He also learned to recognize a good story when he saw one. His image of himself as a writer had now developed into the reality of being a professional; that particular status was to him all-important.

To count as such, Hemingway obviously had to go beyond the lessons learned in Kansas City. He had to create a style of his own, capable of representing events and truths that lie outside the scope of journalism, and to achieve this he had a certain amount of unlearning to do. His companions in journalism were impressed not only by his energy on the job, but also by his interest in literature off the job. The bull's-eye lantern was still burning under his coat.

After working for the *Star* for only six months, Hemingway, then eighteen years old, joined the war in Europe, volunteering for ambulance duty with the American Red Cross in Italy. The newspaper experience had reinforced his natural curiosity and his inclination to be in the thick of things. He was showing the writer's hunger for abundance of material. These traits and acts help to explain the extraordinary richness and precision of his memories of this period. He may have been a tyro still, but he already possessed the true writer's habits of mind.

On the day of his arrival in Milan a munitions factory blew up, and with the other volunteers in his contingent Hemingway was assigned to gathering up the remains of the dead. That incident provided details for his sardonic essay "The Natural History of the Dead." Hemingway's attitude toward war changed at various times in his life, but he never closed his eyes to its horrors.

After a stint of more or less routine ambulance driving at Schio, in the foothills of the Dolomites, he contrived to be assigned to an emergency canteen at Fossalta, on the more active Piave River front facing the Austrians. There, at a forward post, only a month after his arrival in Italy, he was badly wounded in both legs. He was first hit by an Austrian mortar shell and almost immediately after by machine-gun fire—all this in the night—while he was carrying a wounded Italian soldier to safety. This setback marked the beginning of what must have been a very frustrating and painful week: a temporary operation on his legs at a distribution center, five days in a field hospital, and then a grueling train trip to Milan, where he was taken to an American Red Cross hospital for further treatment.

In Milan things took a turn for the better. After successful surgery on his legs he began a slow but sure recovery. He was an authentic war hero to the younger American friends who came to see him. He had been recommended for an Italian medal for valor and had received considerable attention in the press at home as the first American "soldier" to have been wounded in Italy. A photograph of Hemingway taken in his hospital room at this time catches an expression of profound happiness. He had passed a critical test of his mettle with honors. He had also fallen in love with one of the nurses.

Before long he was able to begin outpatient therapy at the Ospedale Maggiore, a routine that provided the physical details and the moods evoked in the haunting short story "In Another Country." In late October he returned briefly to the front as an observer but came down almost immediately with an attack of jaundice and had to return to the Red Cross hospital. By the time he recovered, the Armistice had been signed between Italy and Austria. He remained in Italy for a few more months, visiting friends and trying to keep his wartime romance alive, mostly by letters. Finally, in January, he sailed back to the United States.

Even this bare outline of events covering the period from June 1918 to January 1919 makes clear how mistaken it is to suppose that Hemingway the novelist merely reported experiences without change or invention. It is true that many of the details of the first two parts of *A Farewell to Arms*, published in 1929, probably correspond closely to what had actually occurred, especially the accounts of the wounding of Lieutenant Henry and his hospitalization in Milan. But even in these chapters there are important differences of place, character, and event. For instance, the love affair with the nurse progresses a great deal further in the book than it did in real life. This and other alterations were made in order to create a unified and dramatic story.

The first crisis in Hemingway's writing career occurred after he got home: he was balked in his desire to be a "real" writer, an important writer; the stories he wrote at that time were rejected over and over for a whole year. It is startling to those familiar with Hemingway's later work to read his productions of that period. Their stilted language is utterly unlike what we now know he had it in him to write. He was spinning his wheels. In the straits he was in at that time, it was providential that he managed to add another "Star" to his stardom: he obtained a free-lance job on the Toronto *Star*. Almost a chance event, this was one of the most fortunate opportunities that ever came his way. For a writer there is no substitute for being published and read. The *Star* gave him an appreciative readership and kept him writing on a regular basis. Between February 1920 and December 1924, he wrote over 150 pieces for the *Star*, ranging from amusing sketches of everyday life close to home—medical fads, tips to campers, political satires, and the like—to firsthand observations as a foreign correspondent in postwar Europe.

It was as a foreign correspondent that Hemingway saw his first bullfight in Madrid in 1923. He had made an excursion there from Paris, where he had made his home only a few months after his marriage to Hadley Richardson in 1921. He saw the fight in the company of two friends, Bob McAlmon and Bill Bird, each of whom was soon to publish a collection of Hemingway's writings. According to both men, he was overwhelmed by the bullring experience, so much so that for a time he seemed to talk of nothing else. In fact, bullfighting continued to fascinate him the rest of his life. In 1959, two years before his death, he toured most of Spain following the fights of the matador Antonio Ordoñez and making notes for an article for *Life* magazine on modern bullfighting.

As everybody knows, he was a lifelong sportsman, enthusiastically practicing every sport with which he became familiar. But for Hemingway bullfighting was more than a sport. In his words it was "a tragedy." He was moved, overwhelmed, by the fact that each fight progressed inexorably through separate stages, with the tragic certainty of death for the bull, however brave, and the ever-present risk of death for the man. Every detail of the spectacle captured his imagination: he even observed and recorded the different ways in which people he knew reacted during a bullfight.

Almost immediately after witnessing his first fight he began an exhaustive study of the art, which resulted several years later in his famous treatise *Death in the Afternoon*. He learned about all the current matadors—their lives, their personalities, and the distinctive features of their fighting styles—rating each man with the informed partisanship of an aficionado. He quickly became an expert on the tactics of the bullring and was able to explain them in relation to the natural fighting instincts of the bull, as modified by natural variations in bravery and behavior from one animal to another. In short, he taught himself to think like a bullfighter. He also studied the history of the sport and its economics—the breeding and raising of the bulls, the personal finances of the toreros, and the complex arrangements involved in scheduling the various corridas. He loved the ceremonies and the festival customs and participated wholeheartedly in the spirit of these occasions. In bullfighting he saw a rich source of material for his fiction because the fighting entailed courage and skill.

This intensive study was characteristic of Hemingway. He had a natural, obsessive, and also competitive tendency to find out everything he could about a subject that interested him. He was passionately determined to become an "insider" where so many were satisfied with half-knowledge. It is remarkable how rapidly and thoroughly he was able to educate himself in different fields. Too little attention has been paid by critics to the extraordinary level of his intelligence. He respected knowledge but he respected even more the moral or physical courage of individuals who were willing to stake their careers on what they knew. Hence his admiration for the professionals of bullfighting.

The energetic quest for information was also part of his training as a newspaper correspondent. He sent home both news stories and feature articles, some on special assignment from the *Star*, others that arose out of excursions of his own choosing. This diversity of topics and styles not only broadened his journalistic competence but also gave him the opportunity to meet most of the literary masters who visited or lived in Paris in the twenties—Gertrude Stein, F. Scott Fitzgerald, Ford Madox Ford, James Joyce, Ezra Pound, and Archibald MacLeish.

One of Hemingway's most deeply rooted traits was his horror of being an also-ran. Once he had met writers of stature, it was inevitable that he should try to match or exceed their accomplishments. For a young newspaperman this might have proven a sin of envy deserving to be punished by the gods. But the gods would have been wrong; they had already bestowed on him more than enough talent to fulfill his ambition.

It was during this postwar period that Hemingway tried a number of experiments in the craft of fiction. One of his declared aims was to learn to write "one true sentence." The ministories that were privately published in *In Our Time* were the first fruits of this effort. By stripping off virtually the entire context of an event and leaving a starkly isolated image in a timeless present, Hemingway found that the impact of the words on the reader could be greatly enhanced. Yet it is difficult to measure the success of that new style by the events depicted in this first series of sketches, because the description of executions and other horrors of the battlefield or bullring will in themselves elicit a strong visceral response from the reader—regardless of style.

Fortunately, Hemingway did not stop there. He went on to apply the stripping technique to the mental states of individuals and to the relations between characters. The stories "Up in Michigan" and "Out of Season" are early examples of that "subtractive" technique. The same principle dictated the use of laconic, allusive dialogue. The sparseness of detail forces the reader to pay close attention to whatever information is provided. As a result, the reader's imagination plays an active role and the narrative thereby acquires the convincing force of something worked for and lived through.

Hemingway later used the technique to describe certain aspects of his boyhood, with the clear purpose not so much of retelling as of reproducing the inner feeling of a character at a crucial moment in his life. To what extent Hemingway was influenced by Joyce's method of revealing "epiphanies" in

Dubliners is difficult to establish. I believe that he was so influenced, but such conclusions can often be neither proved nor disproved.

The important element in Hemingway's writings derives from his constant determination to convey powerful psychological states: despair and hope, fear and courage, anger and resignation. Like Conrad, he was primarily concerned with the soul. The story may deal with the body—that is, with exciting action and vivid sensation—but the ultimate goal is to show the transformation of character. Speaking of the famous Hemingway style, Ernest once remarked, "Many writers can learn to write like Papa, but they don't have the same things to say."

Many years ago, in discussing her husband with me, Mary Hemingway told me about his extraordinary ability to walk into a roomful of strangers and instantly divine the multiple relations and attitudes within the group. It is that gift that was responsible for the psychological subtlety of his fiction, a quality that has been overlooked by many readers and critics who take at face value his reputation as a writer concerned primarily with external action.

Given all Hemingway's talents as a writer and the wealth of his experiences traveling through postwar Europe, it was inevitable that he should eventually turn to writing a novel. The inspiration for such a work came to him as the result of a trip to the bullfighting festival at Pamplona in the summer of 1925. He and his wife, Hadley, had made the trip with a group of friends from Paris, and before the excursion was over, there developed a complicated series of dislikes and attractions involving the heroic bullfighter Cayetano Ordoñez. It was perfect material for a novelist, and Hemingway made the most of it in *The Sun Also Rises*. He remodeled the characters as appropriate and changed the sequence of events in order to bring about the explosion touched off in the group by the young matador Pedro Romero. It is interesting to note that no character in the novel corresponds to Hadley Hemingway and that Jake Barnes, whose point of view has been adopted by the author, remains relatively detached from the action and is physically prevented from having an affair with Brett because of a war injury. By this device Hemingway was able to explain the restraints on the conduct of his alter ego in the novel. These inhibitions would not have required special explanation had he presented Jake Barnes, in a role closer to his own experience, as a married man attending the fiesta with his wife, but that note of conventionality would have made the book regrettably different.

In the year following that fiesta, Hemingway's marriage to Hadley began to fall apart. It ended in divorce in 1927, and in May of that year he remarried in Paris. His second wife, Pauline Pfeiffer, had been a friend of both the Hemingways and was the daughter of a wealthy Arkansas family. It was Pauline's millionaire uncle, Gus Pfeiffer, who later not only bought the Hemingways a permanent home in Key West, Florida, but also volunteered to bear all the costs of an African safari for them. In the time of the Great Depression this subsidy amounted to a staggering sum. But between the offer and the safari itself a number of things caused postponements. Hemingway had three years in which to look forward to it, with some impatience.

For two of the intervening summers—1930 and 1932—the Hemingways lived on a dude ranch in northwestern Wyoming, beside the Clarks Fork branch of the Yellowstone River. There Hemingway was able to get some experience with big game on hunting trips for mountain sheep, elk, and bear. He also had a chance to try out the big Springfield rifle that had been made to order for the safari.

He was a born hunter. His father had taught him to use a rifle and a shotgun, and despite poor eyesight later necessitating glasses, Ernest became a fine shot with both weapons. Dr. Hemingway preached the wrongness of killing for the sake of killing and insisted that one should eat any animal one shot. In later life Hemingway did not always comply with that rule, but he did not forget it either. He believed without question that hunting had its own morality. In an article written for *Esquire* during a safari, he distinguished between "shootism" and "sport" on just such grounds.

Another side of Hemingway as a hunter was his competitiveness. He fought this tendency in himself and usually tried to conceal it, seldom with complete success. When his Key West friend, Charles Thompson, came out to Wyoming in 1932 to hunt, their trips had a way of turning into contests. Thompson was also invited on the African safari the following year. He appears as Karl in *Green Hills of Africa*, the novel Hemingway wrote about a safari. When the book opens, near the end of the safari, Karl has outshone the protagonist consistently in the size and quality of his big-game trophies. The latter is attempting to even up the score somewhat by killing a better kudu than Karl's. More or less on the sidelines are the other members of the party: Pauline (P.O.M. or Poor Old Mama), the white hunter Philip Percival (Jackson Phillips or Pop), and his assistant Ben Fourie (Dan). The African gunbearers, drivers, and trackers appear with their own names or nicknames. The campsite was in eastern Tanganyika, off the road to Handeni. Hemingway's first African safari would have almost as great an impact on his life and writing as the discovery of Spain and bullfighting had ten years earlier. The whole adventure lasted not much more than ten weeks, but his consciousness was so stimulated by his enthusiasm and curiosity that every event seems to have been indelibly etched in his memory. The wealth of their detail creates the impression of a much longer time in Africa than Hemingway actually spent.

During the expedition Hemingway often talked with Philip Percival about the latter's experiences as a white hunter. He was gathering as much information as possible about the sport. A hunter of dangerous game sometimes faced formidable risks, especially if he abided by the rules of the sport: to shoot only on foot and to hunt down a wounded animal in order to dispatch it humanely. Situations could arise on a safari that called for courage, and, as we know, Hemingway was profoundly interested in that particular trait, in itself and in relation to pride and fear.

A brave man may lose his courage in special circumstances, and a coward may find courage suddenly and unexpectedly. War and the bullring had provided Hemingway with examples of such lightning changes, and he was discovering others in discussions with Percival as well as in his own new experience.

Although factual and autobiographical, *Green Hills of Africa* was designed to have the same psychological effect on his readers as a work of the imagination. Hemingway rearranged the sequence of the events accordingly, constructing the scenes of each part with that purpose in mind.

It is worth commenting on Hemingway's honesty as a writer: he revealed with the utmost candor his feelings of envy and frustration, however much he may have tried not to show those emotions during the action itself. It is, of course, this underlying contest between him and Karl that gives the story its suspense. Hemingway's artistic intention ruled first and last. Writers are sometimes criticized for being self-centered. What else can they be if they are to take advantage of the material provided by their own emotions? Tolstoy, whom Hemingway admired as a novelist, was the great master of that kind of self-exploitation.

The Spanish Civil War was a crucial event in Hemingway's life. For almost two years it absorbed his whole attention and led to some of his finest work as a writer. Several things combined to make that war important to him: his love of Spain and the Spanish people, his fear and hatred of fascism, his interest in war itself, the journalistic attraction of a "big story," and, as a compound of all these things, the impact of his life in Spain on his creative imagination.

Hemingway's strong sympathy for the Loyalist cause did not prevent him from portraying the people he saw as they really were or from showing what they actually did. This reveals something very important about Hemingway as a writer: he was strongly committed to the truth. His conscience as an artist forced him to hold a point of view above any particular party line and to maintain a corresponding impartiality in seeing the good and the bad in individuals on both sides. During the Spanish war political views were strongly polarized, and Hemingway was later criticized by the Left for writing about excesses on the Loyalist side. But the criticism did not influence his point of view. It could be fairly said about Hemingway's writing what Tolstoy once said about his own: that its hero was the truth.

Although Hemingway wrote from experience, he had to depict a cast of authentically Spanish men and women who were relatively isolated from the foreigners who had taken their side. This posed a special problem: How should these characters speak? He did not want to try rendering their speech by idiomatic English. Instead, he devised a special idiom that would convey the construction and flavor of the original Spanish. Although this device has been criticized as artificial, a good case can be made for it on the grounds that a thought framed and spoken in Spanish often has no precise equivalent in spoken English. Particularly when writing about simple people whose thoughts have been largely shaped by their language, it is reasonable for the author to try to find some way of catching their characteristic expressions.

Finally, Hemingway's love of deep-sea fishing and his involvement with the sea became major interests in his life. Several of the articles he wrote in the thirties deal with adventures on his thirty-eight-foot craft, the *Pilar*. He often took groups of friends on excursions to Havana or Bimini for fishing in the Gulf Stream. He threw himself into the sport with his usual gusto and thoroughness, and as usual he passed on to readers what he had learned and done, along with his personal theories, such as that about the natural history of the marlin. "The Great Blue River," written for *Holiday* in 1949, is a later article in that vein. It describes a day of marlin fishing by Hemingway and Mary, and its lively, informative account shows him at his happiest. But his masterpiece of marine writing is the novella *The Old Man and the Sea*, published three years later. Part of its power comes from bringing together so many of the themes of Hemingway's best work: his love of the sea, his tragic view of the contest between a brave man and a brave animal, his respect for the endurance and instinctive courage of simple people, and his compassion for the trials of old age. Rarely has so short a work held an emotional charge of such magnitude. More than any other story it seems to have given Hemingway a means of expressing his deepest beliefs about life.

The idea for the story had been planted in his mind almost by chance when, years before, he was told a story about an old Cuban fisherman in a small boat who had killed a giant marlin after a similar struggle, only to lose it to the sharks. Hemingway retold this anecdote in a paragraph of one of his articles for *Esquire* in 1936, "On the Blue Water: A Gulf Stream Letter." Thereafter the idea lay dormant. In 1939 he mentioned it in a letter to Maxwell Perkins as the subject of a story he intended to write. But it was not until early in 1951 that he began the actual composition. It was finished in a little over a month.

Immediately after its publication *The Old Man and the Sea* became a major success, critically and commercially. It was specifically referred to in the citation accompanying the author's Nobel Prize for Literature in 1954. Of all the praise the book received, the comment that pleased the author most was made by the art historian Bernard Berenson:

> Hemingway's *The Old Man and the Sea* is an idyll of the sea as sea, as un-Byronic and un-Melvillian as Homer himself, and communicated in prose as calm and compelling as Homer's verse. No real artist symbolizes or allegorizes—and Hemingway is a real artist—but every real work of art exhales symbols and allegories. So does this short but not small masterpiece.

It was *The Sun Also Rises* that brought Hemingway together in 1926 with his future editor Maxwell Perkins, although their meeting took place in a roundabout way. The two men hit it off from the start. Their introduction resulted in Hemingway's accepting a contract covering not only the unfinished text of *The Sun Also Rises* but also his novella *The Torrents of Spring*, which was published first.

For Perkins, that contract was the successful upshot of a long campaign to bring the talented young author onto the Scribner list. A year earlier, upon the strenuous urging of Scott Fitzgerald, Max had written to Hemingway in Europe asking him to submit his work to Scribners. But by the time the letter reached Hemingway in Paris, the writer had already signed up with Boni and Liveright in New York. That firm published Hemingway's first book-length collection of short stories under the title *In Our Time*. Hemingway's contract with Boni and Liveright gave the publisher an option on his second book and, if accepted, on his third. As it turned out, Boni and Liveright published neither. It turned down *The Torrents of Spring*, seeing the novel as too clearly a parody of its famous author Sherwood Anderson. The rejection must have been particularly painful for Horace Liveright, who must have felt that he had earned the right to be Hemingway's publisher. But what could he do? To Perkins, on the other hand, it was an unexpected reversal of fortune. He was now able to sign up a promising writer at the cost of publishing a relatively minor work. As it turned out and as I mentioned, Perkins was also taking on a "life-long author." Today, when so many writers change publishers with as little hesitation as they might change newsdealers, Hemingway's loyalty seems ever more extraordinary.

During the first twenty years or so of Hemingway's association with Scribners, Max Perkins was his principal link with the company. It was to Perkins that he wrote continually about his writing projects, his books, his travels, his ideas, his family, and his finances. Perkins was wholly devoted to Hemingway, an entirely trustworthy friend and confidant as well. At the same time, he maintained a degree of professional detachment that Hemingway preferred to a more effusive relationship. They were both shy men, though their shyness took different forms. In a situation where Hemingway might become boisterous, Perkins would more likely withdraw into his shell. Besides, Perkins was hard of hearing, an affliction not entirely a handicap for a book editor.

During the thirties and forties Hemingway came to know other members of the Scribners editorial team. After the deaths of Perkins and of my father, Wallace Meyer became Hemingway's editor. Hemingway generally got along well with his editors but tended to distrust the company's sales and business officers. He imagined that they did not understand or appreciate his writings and that they were not wholly committed to promoting his books. He later admitted to me that most writers seem to have impaired eyesight when it comes to seeing advertisements for their books.

By the 1940s a close friendship had developed between Hemingway and my father. Their relationship was strengthened by occasional luncheons and dinner parties in New York and Paris and by visits to Finca Vigia, Hemingway's farm in Cuba. It was during a visit there that my father first had the chance to read in manuscript large portions of *For Whom the Bell Tolls.* Later, and with perhaps a trace of irony in his deference, Hemingway asked my father to check the passages about horses in the first part of the novel. It was—as always—important to Ernest that such details be technically correct. Later he wrote my father a letter filled with details of horse anatomy so minute that it would have astonished a veterinarian. He insisted on being the expert, yet he also kept teasing my father for being so wrapped up in horses. On one occasion he tried to horrify him by filling a letter with the gory details of his running over a horse when driving a car. How much of that incident was horse feathers I shall leave to others to determine. It made a good story.

Although my father did not pretend to be a man of letters, Hemingway valued his naturally sound literary perceptions and his consistently active common sense. My father slipped easily into the role of Hemingway's chief link with Scribners when Perkins died in 1947. The two men entered almost at once into a voluminous correspondence in which they kidded and insulted each other in a way that bespoke a deep mutual affection. For example, my father would write, "I have just received your cheerful but rather vulgar letter" or would say to his famous author, "I had hoped you might have matured more over the years."

Because so many accounts of Hemingway's behavior depict him as churlish or capricious, I should like to comment on his amiability toward both Max and my father. Before Hemingway admitted anyone into his inner circle, he needed to trust him to an abnormal degree, and this individual had to adhere unswervingly to Hemingway's image of him. His trust once given, he would ease into a friendly informality, indeed a boyish camaraderie. He enjoyed having his own gang. On the other hand, when Ernest dealt with persons he was not sure of or who had an ax to grind, he was prone to truculence in self-protection. He did not like or dislike anyone half-heartedly.

When I joined Scribners in the mid forties, Perkins was still editor in chief, and I was fortunate to have almost a year in which to see him in action. I had been put in charge of publicity and advertising, but my father and Max had a way of giving me other publishing chores that I was usually unqualified to handle. Scribners had espoused the sink-or-swim method of instruction, and it was not always easy to stay afloat.

One of my assignments was to supervise the production of an illustrated edition of *A Farewell to Arms*. It is still not clear to me why that item was placed on my plate, but there were difficulties about the book, the biggest and clearest being that Hemingway did not care for the illustrations. Perhaps it was believed that this hot potato might do less damage to an innocent newcomer like myself, who was not responsible for its conception. In any case, I set about proofreading the text and performing other tasks, little realizing that I was dealing with a potential *casus belli*. When the time came I wrote to our famous author and gave him a deadline for the introduction he had agreed to write for the book. In due course he sent it to me. The introduction was written in an *"O tempora, o mores"* vein, denouncing war. As for the illustrations, he scarcely mentioned them at all, except to describe the disappointment they caused him. He made no bones about that and spoke wistfully about how he would have preferred an artist like Winslow Homer or Renoir.

In his accompanying letter to me, he brushed aside any concerns I might have about publishing his introduction. I was not to worry about the feelings of the illustrator; illustrators have no right to have feelings, ranking little higher than photographers. I was also not to worry that what he wrote was politically subversive. His folks had been around a long time. They had all done their duty in time of war. Hemingway was not a pen name. He could take an oath that he had never been a member of the Communist party. He was not being snotty, he added, just kidding rough the way he did with my old man. It was vintage Hemingway, a grand mixture of wild hyperbole and sweeping decrees. It was fun to read, and I also felt the implicit friendliness in his treating me in the same confiding way that he used with my father.

I did not hear from Hemingway again until four years later when he wrote to me about my father's sudden death in February 1952. I had been called back into the navy and was stationed in Washington. In his letter, Hemingway wanted me to know how bad he felt about having been away and out of touch when my father died, and that, since he had to die, at least he had gotten it over with. As for myself, Ernest said I did not have to write him letters or have him on my mind. I cannot imagine a kinder expression of condolence or a more delicate assurance of loyalty. And in the lovely phrase of Dickens, he was better than his word. For the next nine years of his life, he was as easy to work with as any author I have ever known.

When I was released from active navy duty a month or so after these events and exchanges, I returned to New York as president of the company. Wallace Meyer was still Hemingway's editor, and all of us were looking forward to publishing *The Old Man and the Sea*. We had no doubt of its virtuosity. I was proceeding with a scheme to bring all of Hemingway's books back onto the Scribner list, for, as I noted earlier, most of the titles had been licensed for hardcover reprints by the Modern Library or Grosset and Dunlap, or again for paperback reprints by Bantam and others. I had a master plan, and I wrote Ernest the following letter outlining it:

> I have asked for a complete report on the publishing status of all your titles because I wanted to be certain that nothing was sold on a reprint basis that might be sold by us on terms conceivably more remunerative to you.
>
> Frankly I am attempting to provide for the effects that the publication of *The Old Man and the Sea* could have on all your earlier works. We anticipate a wonderful reception to this such as would have to follow the publication of something so magnificent.

I do not think that my crystal ball is better than that of any other publisher, but I must admit that it was never so helpful as on that occasion. Hemingway endorsed my plan wholeheartedly, even though it called for the cancellation of Modern Library editions to which he had strong sentimental attachments. Over the next few years we reissued all his books, first in hardcover and then in paperback for school and college use. We redesigned the bindings, reset some of the older books, and redid almost all the jackets.

Hemingway was delighted by this systematic revival of his books. He disagreed with our suggestions only once or twice, and then only in the most tactful manner. For example, he took exception to a drawing of a bullfighter for the jacket of *Death in the Afternoon* and wrote me as follows: "It has this against it, Charlie: the bullfighter is a Mexican, an Indian, and he looks almost as though he were suffering from leprosy in the peculiar swellings of his face." We scrapped that jacket and afterwards managed to have an Ektachrome photograph taken of the original of the Roberto Domingo poster at the Finca. Another time one of our book designers thought it would be a good idea to print the interchapter pieces of *In Our Time* in red ink instead of in italics. Hemingway was very doubtful about that idea: "My mother at one time had some theory about transcribing music into color but I never subscribed to it."

The correspondence between Hemingway and me now belongs to Princeton and is preserved in the Firestone Library. Before I reread those letters, I remembered Hemingway as being very kind to me as a young man from the time of our first contacts over thirty years before. But that impression did not prepare me for the extraordinary warmth and kindness of his letters. I am much older now and have a better idea of the value of kindness.

The Hemingway that I dealt with professionally was as magnanimous as any man I ever met. Most of my letters were written in a practical vein and involved business matters. I did not feel it would be appropriate for me to seek or to expect the easy footing of intimate friendship that had existed between Hemingway and Perkins or between Hemingway and my father. I think he understood that and was all the more gracious. Occasionally he wrote in a paternal vein, giving me curious rules for life. The first was straightforward: "Always do sober what you said you'd do when you were drunk. That will teach you to keep your mouth shut." The other two were cryptic: "Never fool around with bears" and "Never do knife tricks." What possibly painful mishaps with bears and knives did he have in youth?

Of course there were occasional contretemps. One of the most instructive was in connection with *The Old Man and the Sea*. A young college traveler for Scribners discovered the story's embryonic *Esquire* version I spoke of earlier. For all I know, the man may have been told about the *Esquire* piece by one of the English professors he had called on. That young man is now a prominent literary agent—and what more can he desire from life? But it occurred to him that it would be an admirable thing to republish this *Ur*-version of *The Old Man and the Sea*, together with the novella itself, in a special college edition. We thought it was a pretty good idea too and proposed it to Ernest. But Hemingway—Hemingway the writer—did not think it a good idea at all. Indeed, I shall remember Hemingway's fury at the suggestion.

Why was he so put out? Until recently I ascribed this to his well-known resentment of scholars who ferreted out his sources or explored his life. In these matters he was apt to express the combined disbelief and rage of a magician when someone in the audience keeps explaining his feats. Now I think I have a sharper understanding of Ernest's annoyance. For Hemingway, his story had an outside and an inside: the outside might be the basis for a good yarn—and so it was in *Esquire*—but the inside was the basis for a work of literature.

I suppose the greatest strain on our relationship arose when I asked him to write an introduction for a paperback collection of his stories. This was in 1959, and Hemingway worked at it very conscientiously in Spain during May and June. When the piece came in I was shocked by its tone and contents. It would have been a disservice to his reputation to publish it, especially for student use, and I saw no alternative but to bite the bullet and tell him so. I now suspect that there was an earth tremor in that part of Spain when my letter arrived. On July 3 I received a cable ordering me to stop work on the anthology and on all similar projects. It had been a big mistake that he would not make again. Although the cable ended with "kind regards," I was terribly worried that I had ruined my relationship with Hemingway.

A month later he wrote to me again, saying he was sorry about the school project not coming off. He had really taken it seriously and tried to write something that would counteract the type of teaching that children were getting on the short story form. Mary did not like it either. He was happy to have me try the alternative plan I had outlined for selling the books and would go along with me completely. With the confidence he had in me as a publisher, he said, that was a very easy decision to make. He concluded by saying, "If I can't write for you anymore, I'll be your scout."

During the years I corresponded with Hemingway we did not meet more than four or five times, all those meetings being in New York City. The first was in June 1953, when my wife, Joan, and I went to the pier to see Ernest and Mary off on the *Flandre* on the first leg of their trip to France, Spain, and Africa.

We waited for them rather self-consciously in their stateroom, together with other visitors whom we knew only by name. Ominous bells and horns were sounding continually, and it seemed likely that the ship would set sail with us on board and not the Hemingways. We had almost given up hope when the cabin door burst open and in plunged Hemingway, with a large retinue bringing up the rear. There was now no room to turn around, and the air turned blue with four-letter words and Hemingwayisms.

Ernest's lawyer Alfred Rice had brought some important documents that needed to be signed, but Hemingway pretended to brush them off as trivialities. He was delighted by the wisecrack he had heard that Hollywood was going to change the name of the Spencer Tracy film from *The Old Man and the Sea* to *The Old Jew and the Lake*; he kept repeating this despite the fact that the actor himself was close by. It seemed certain now that the last call for visitors to go ashore had long since been given, but with all the loud talking no one could have heard it.

In the midst of this confusion Hemingway even took time out to inscribe for me a copy of the limited edition of his novella with the slogan *"Il faut d'abord durer."* Although we finally did disembark in New York and not in Le Havre, our visit made me realize the appropriateness of this latest Hemingway slogan about the necessity to endure. It was no small feat to survive the strain of many such performances. Nothing in his letters had given me an inkling of the frenzied pace of those incidents of his life.

I did not see Hemingway again until six years later, in November of 1959. He had just returned to New York on the *Liberté* and was staying for a few days in a borrowed apartment on the East Side. His friend George Plimpton called me at my office and said, "Your famous author is in town and wants to see you." I hurried over.

It was the briefest of meetings, mostly filled with small talk. I do not drink, and when I declined a highball, Ernest suggested a vermouth and soda. It was virtually not drinking, he said, but it does light a little fire. I found that an appealing phrase, but I stuck to ginger ale.

One of the difficulties of visiting Hemingway in New York was that he was almost always surrounded by well-wishers. Each of them appeared to believe that he or she had the special responsibility of protecting Ernest from the others, which generated a fair degree of tension. It was, moreover, difficult to conduct a serious conversation.

Because our friendship had been created almost entirely through letters, it was probably natural that I felt barely familiar with him on a face-to-face basis. A few days after this encounter he delivered to me, courtesy of A. E. Hotchner, some first drafts of his "Paris Sketches," which we were to publish posthumously under the title *A Moveable Feast*. Naturally, we read them at once, and because we were so positively impressed by them I called Ernest immediately to tell him so. I was astonished to hear him respond like a diffident young writer having a book accepted for the first time. He was obviously delighted. "I thought you'd be willing to lend me money on the strength of this," he said. Of course we would gladly have lent him all the money he wished, but he had never borrowed any. That was just his way of expressing his pleasure.

The next meeting with him was in an apartment he had rented on Sixty-second Street. Our editor Harry Brague and I went over to find out when he wished to publish the "Paris Sketches." Hemingway's health was very poor, and he agonized over the question in a way that made me sad. I wished we had not raised the question. He worried about the effect on his eyes of having to work on a book. How would he be able to shoot a gun if he couldn't see? Would he have to learn to shoot by ear? As it turned out, these "Paris Sketches" were the first of several posthumous works and collections, all of which were received in a way that would have filled Hemingway with joy.

At the end of that visit, he gave me a battered valise to take back to the office and hold for him under lock and key. He mentioned that it contained his will. "Don't lose it," he told me. I knew he had had some terrible experiences with lost suitcases in the past, so I reassured him as well as I could.

Very early the next morning, Ernest appeared at Scribners. He wanted to look something up among the papers he had given me. I opened the locked filing cabinet outside my office and watched him rummage around in the valise. I realized, of course, that he had come to Scribners only to make sure I hadn't lost it. He then came into my office all cheerful. That was the occasion when, to put me at my ease, he sat down in my chair. I stood there quite at a loss, not knowing where to sit, feeling rather disoriented. We offered him some coffee, and one of the secretaries brought in a cup with a great sense of mission. "Would you like some cream?" we asked. "Just enough to change the color," he replied with characteristic precision. He added detailed instructions for pouring in the cream. Only Hemingway would have thought out a specific formula for this commonplace operation. It was a kind of summary of his approach to life—accuracy, simplicity, and style.

We exchanged letters afterwards, but that was the last time I saw Ernest.

II

Reflections on
Reading and Writing

Appreciating the
English Language

இ

In the 1960s I had the privilege of lunching with the distinguished classicist Gilbert Highet. At one point in our conversation I asked him how one could explain the dramatic decline in the quality of Roman literature in the generations following the so-called Augustan and Silver ages. Professor Highet's answer was simple, but not one I had expected. The literature declined, he said, because the language deteriorated. Now this is an explanation that gives one something to think about! How about our own age? Is language deteriorating? How does a language deteriorate? Will much of our literature be thought of as decadent? By what standards does one make such a judgment? There are no pat answers to questions like these.

Often when one watches television, with all its studied vulgarity of language and thought and feeling, one believes indeed that we are well into a new dark age. And one becomes even more pessimistic when one listens to some of our well-educated people, who should know better, willfully adopting a manner of speech that makes Pidgin English sound almost Shakespearean. But how representative are these excesses? It is difficult to be certain.

About one thing I feel very certain, and that is that a language does not deteriorate simply because it changes. Languages have always metamorphosed in the course of time, at different rates it is true, but no living language ever remains static. Both the meanings of the words and their frequency of use shift, and old syntactical forms evolve into new ones. Despite the ferocious convictions of some English teachers to the contrary, there can never be a permanent model for so-called correct usage. Much of present-day English would have horrified our ancestors and vice versa.

But we cannot allow the inevitability of change to make us complacent about the direction it will take. Indeed, the preservation of a rich and expressive language like ours is as important to the life of the mind as clean air and clean water are to our physical well-being. If we persist in contaminating American English by mindless jargon, puerile slang, and perverse usage, and if we continue to neglect its resources by failing or refusing to cultivate them, we shall pay a high price.

Today there are friends of the earth and friends of wildlife, friends of the redwoods and friends of wolves and whales. It would seem that the time has come to recruit friends of English. There is certainly no lack of work to be done if we are to restore adequate standards of literacy. Today's students need to know that studying their language and learning to write well are of immense value to the individual throughout life and to the society he or she hopes to serve. It is important that students know this fact, for the future of English—indeed, the future of everything else we cherish—depends on them as our posterity.

Any diminishment of the logical clarity or evocative power of our language is a serious loss, not only to our ability to express our thoughts effectively but also our ability to form our thoughts. Language itself is very close to the essence of humanness. Man is unique among mammals by reason of his virtuosity in using signs. Actually, the ability to develop a language is probably the result of a specific change or changes in the structure of the human brain—it required hundreds of thousands of years of biological evolution. Similarly, all the various languages of man have required centuries of cultural evolution. Each of us was born with an enormous natural capacity to learn and use a language, but we were born with no more of an inherited language than a prehistoric child. We face the loss of eons of effort if we let our language deteriorate.

In thinking about language we are often handicapped by being too close to the subject. Conveying our ideas in words is so familiar and habitual an activity that it requires conscious effort for us to look at our language from the outside. Words are among the first sounds we hear in the cradle, and it is natural that they should seem a fixed part of reality, like sound itself.

Even as adults we need to be reminded that a familiar word like *table* is, in spoken form, a combination of sounds associated with the idea of a table only by convention, and that the word in its written form is likewise a conventional way of transcribing the sounds. Familiarity and habit make it easy for us to forget that all languages are essentially artifacts—that is, traditional codes used to convey or record human thought.

We can trace the origins of writing in its modern form to the simple alphabet developed by the Phoenicians, and beyond that to the earlier and more complex forms used by the Babylonians and Egyptians, and beyond those again to prehistoric pictograms. About the origins of language one can only speculate.

It is possible that oral communication was actually an invention of prehistoric man, developed and ramified over hundreds of thousands of years. It is hard to imagine such an invention. Even the most primitive peoples possess elaborate languages, and we tend to take speech for granted as a biological rather than a cultural endowment. Yet some may find inspiration in the thought that learning to speak was one of the earliest, and certainly the greatest, achievements of man. The thoughtful might thus come to treasure their language as a legacy from an awesomely distant past.

Another belief that we accept without thinking is that our own language lies at the center of the linguistic universe. Some people seem to find it strange that there are other languages at all. Mark Twain made fun of that attitude in *Huckleberry Finn* when he described Huck's futile attempts to convince Jim that a Frenchman can be human even if he does not speak English. How can the French understand what they are saying?

A good way of stepping outside one's own language and looking at it objectively is to learn a foreign one. It is a fact, paradoxical as it may seem, that studying two languages makes mastery of both easier. Yet it is as true of language study as of most other studies that the insights acquired by analysis, as in translating from one language to another, are as necessary for proficiency as are the intuitions instilled by habit and drill.

In the days when most high school students took Latin, the strangeness of that language was the very means by which the function of words in English was brought out: it separated function from meaning. Thus the grammars of the two languages could be learned simultaneously. A further advantage of studying Latin lies in the fact that a host of English words have Latin roots and disclose their meaning by knowledge of their origins. This is also true of a small number of Greek words, like *heterodox* and *hypodermic*.

Another good way of breaking out of our linguistic shell is to learn something of the history of the English language. The argument for it is the same as the one that justifies historical research in any field: a knowledge of the origin and development of a human institution is the first step toward understanding its nature and gauging its present value.

For the beginner's purposes a survey of the English language need not go into detail or strive for scrupulous precision. The important thing is to give the student a grasp of the subject and to capture his imagination by its picturesqueness. The student should come away permanently curious about word origins and knowledgeable enough to grasp the etymologies in a dictionary and use them in enlarging his vocabulary. This practice will automatically teach how languages evolve in the course of time, either accumulating small variations or more rapidly by merging and borrowing, when two peoples speaking different languages come into close social and political contact, whether friendly or hostile. At the same time, the student will come to see the interrelations between the oral and written traditions.

Virtually all the elementary parts of speech in English are of Anglo-Saxon derivation. This includes the articles, pronouns, conjunctions, and prepositions, as well as the various forms of the verbs *to be* and *to have*. The same source supplied a great many words denoting familiar, everyday things: nouns like *wind, bird, tree,* and *house;* adjectives like *strong, little, green,* and *old;* and verbs like *to blow, to fly, to stand,* and *to own.* If we take a few lines from some well-known poem and circle all the Anglo-Saxon derivatives, we can see the frequency of these derivations in the English language and at the same time gain a sense of their ancient past. Try this with Shelley's "Ode to a Skylark."

The history of English is filled with instructive examples of the interaction of political and linguistic forces. During the six hundred years from the Germanic occupation of England around A.D. 450 to the Norman Conquest in 1066, the language of the Anglo-Saxons developed along a relatively uninterrupted course despite outside influences. The conversion of the whole population to Christianity in the seventh century introduced them to Latin as the language of the Church and at the same time taught them the authority and value of a written tradition. It was at that early date that a number of Latin words supplemented or replaced Germanic ones in the Anglo-Saxon vocabulary. For example, the Anglo-Saxon word *mont* was probably introduced then from the Latin word *mons* (*montis*), meaning a mountain or hill. It survives in present-day English as *mount*, while its Germanic equivalent *berg* has remained in our vocabulary only in the word *iceberg*. It is interesting that the Anglo-Saxons did not adopt the Latin word for "gospel," *evangelium*, but instead translated it literally into their own language as *godspel*, meaning "good tidings." Was the Latin word too difficult for them to pronounce?

A violent chapter in Anglo-Saxon history began in the latter part of the eighth century when bands of Danes began to raid the east coast of England, plundering villages and terrorizing the inhabitants. These sporadic Viking attacks culminated in a full-scale invasion toward the end of the ninth century. In the battles that ensued, the Danes succeeded in conquering almost all of England and establishing permanent settlements in many parts that had been Anglo-Saxon kingdoms.

For the next two hundred years the two peoples lived in adjacent territories. They were often in conflict with one another, and in the early part of the eleventh century one war between them ended with the Danes placing a Danish king on the English throne. But despite their prolonged contact with the Anglo-Saxons, the Danes did not contribute a great many of their own words to the English language. Rather, they tended to adopt the language of the Anglo-Saxons, closely enough related to their own. Indeed, the similarity of the two languages makes it difficult now to be certain whether a particular Norse word may not have belonged to an Anglo-Saxon dialect.

But some Scandinavian contributions to the English vocabulary have been identified, including such familiar words as *anger, awe, egg, sky, lake,* and *law.* It is also known that the endings *-by, -thorp,* and *-thwaite,* in the names of certain English towns—Whitby, Althorp, and Braithwaite, for example—are derived from the Old Norse words for "town," "village," and "clearing," respectively. Thus the word *bylaw* is derived from the Scandinavian word meaning "town law."

In the ninth and tenth centuries political events in England resulted in a standardizing of the language. The Saxon kingdom of Wessex took supremacy over all the other Anglo-Saxon kingdoms not ruled by the Danes, and the dialect of the West Saxons became the language of government for the "English" nation. This simultaneous political and linguistic unification had social and cultural consequences that are important to bear in mind today, when so many persons are inclined to accept, if not promote, linguistic pluralism within our own nation.

The utility of the common language for maintaining common government and common rights of citizenship can be seen not only in what I have just pointed out about Anglo-Saxon England, but also in the history of virtually every major nation. A present-day example is the unifying force of the English language in India. And think of the disturbing negative case of Quebec French, which may yet result in dividing Canada.

In England in the tenth century, the establishment of Anglo-Saxon as the official language of the nation also made possible the development of a national literature, and this in turn contributed to the further standardizing of the language and the extension of its use. While only a small portion of the prose and poetry of the period remains, what has survived is impressive.

Had the English nation kept its independence in the ensuing centuries, its language would have remained relatively stable and very different from the one we use today. As it happened, the Norman Conquest of England in the middle of the eleventh century completely overturned the country's political life. In the social upheaval that followed, Anglo-Saxon was demoted to the language of a subservient people; native speakers reverted to several different dialects, and literature came to an end.

For more than two centuries following the Norman Conquest, England was a bilingual country, a situation that was bound to affect both languages. In the early part of his novel *Ivanhoe* (once required reading for every American high school student), Walter Scott dramatized these social distinctions of the time by showing the language differences between the two parts of the population: master spoke Norman French and servant some form of Anglo-Saxon. As a result, profound changes took place in Anglo-Saxon. The loss of a standard dialect and of a continued literary tradition multiplied linguistic variations. Many of the old inflections and constructions were either simplified or dropped. All these modifications brought the language closer to the forms and structure of modern English, at the same time as the use of numerous French words entered the everyday speech of the common people. The swineherd Gurth in *Ivanhoe* would have known and used such words as *baron, duke, court, castle,* and *dungeon,* which the Normans had made a part of everyday life.

The future of this importation of French into England was also determined by circumstance, but of a different sort. As long as the noblemen of Norman descent felt themselves to be Norman first and English second, they continued to use French as the primary language of the Church, the law courts, and their own homes. But this allegiance to their origins inevitably weakened from generation to generation. French had been a foreign language for the Norman's own ancestors, the Norsemen who had conquered northern France in the tenth century and soon borrowed the language of that region. With the passage of time, the dialect of French spoken in England came to be regarded on the Continent as a more and more outmoded patois. The decisive break occurred in the middle of the thirteenth century, when the English Crown lost its land and possessions in France. From then on, the ruling classes in England thought of that country as their homeland and were willing to adopt English as the language of government. In the course of a few generations the displacement of French was practically complete.

But it was a different English that was now established as the chief language of the nation. Its vocabulary was virtually doubled by the use of the French words familiar to a large part of the population. Some of these French terms replaced the Anglo-Saxon ones, some became synonyms, and some conveyed new ideas. The French words tended to reflect the customs and interests of an educated aristocracy. They included words belonging to the language of the law and the Church, of literature and scholarship, chivalry and manners. They made it possible to convey in English abstractions and shades of meaning absent from the Anglo-Saxon vocabulary. The result of combining the two languages was their eventual fusion into a single language of extraordinary richness, vigor, and beauty.

The presence in the English language of so many French words—a good many of which stemmed from classical Latin—made it easy and natural to Anglicize Latin and Greek words by bringing them directly into the language with only minor modifications. That took place on a large scale with the revival of learning from the fourteenth through the sixteenth centuries; scholars and writers "Latinized" English by massive borrowings from the ancient classics. Shakespeare's exuberant phrase "the multitudinous seas incarnadine" exemplifies that fashion of the period.

In some cases the same Latin word was represented by two English words, one coming into the language indirectly through medieval French and one entering directly from the Latin. *Dainty* and *dignity,* both derived from the Latin *dignitas,* and *poor* and *pauper* from the Latin *pauper* are examples of such dual words, called "doublets." In many instances, as in the first pair, the two words now have clearly different meanings.

In Shakespeare's lifetime the English-speaking people constituted a realm of approximately five million inhabitants. While it was natural that Shakespeare should use English in writing popular plays for London audiences, learned authors of the time, such as the English philosopher Francis Bacon, wrote in Latin as a matter of course. They were forced to if they wanted a large readership outside their own country. Latin was the international language of learning in the Renaissance, as it had been throughout the Middle Ages.

In Bacon's time and for about a century after him, few would have been rash enough to prophesy that one day the language of Shakespeare would become preeminent throughout the world and would replace Latin as the second language of educated persons. Yet that is what has taken place in the twentieth century. It was recently estimated that English is the mother tongue of close to one-third billion persons, and in countries with other native tongues as many persons again are studying English in schools or using it in their everyday life.

We recognize now that, at the time of Shakespeare's death in 1616, certain historical facts and events presaged the future importance of English. In India the British East India Company had succeeded in establishing a trading station in Surat. That was one seed of the British Empire, which by the middle of the nineteenth century ruled colonies all over the world. Already English-speaking dominions existed in Canada, New Zealand, and Australia. Again in 1616 a tiny settlement of the New World, in Jamestown, was struggling to survive, and that was the embryonic beginning of an English-speaking nation that has become one of the world's foremost powers, numbering today some 250 million inhabitants.

As one might expect, the contacts of English-speaking peoples with those speaking different languages resulted in the addition of innumerable foreign words to the English language. Many have become so familiar that it comes as a shock to learn their origins: from Hindi we have taken the word *thug,* from Japanese *tycoon,* from Gaelic *hooligan,* from Czech *robot,* and from the Dutch *skipper.* World War I contributed the French word *camouflage.* World War II added the Gaelic word *gremlin* to the English language.

The rise of modern science and technology flooded the language with new terminology. Indeed, special dictionaries are needed to cover the vocabularies of the scientific disciplines. In these fields it has been the practice to borrow or coin new words from Latin or Greek. In physics, for example, we find the Latin words *momentum* and *inertia* as well as the Greek derivatives *entropy* and *thermodynamics.* Medicine, which has a tradition of speaking in Latin, has in fact some equivalents made up from either language: for example, *malnutrition* from the Latin and *dystrophy* from the Greek. In chemistry the names of important compounds have become so long as to be unpronounceable. The molecule of deoxyribonucleic acid is of such fundamental importance that it is commonly referred to as DNA.

Because scientific terms sound so mysterious and authoritative to the laity, quack medicine and other pseudosciences, as well as business and advertising, have copied the jargon and filled the language with absurd compounds: *hydramatic transmission* and *analgesic action* are but a duo among a multitude. It remains to be seen whether the language can survive these trends.

Although a few purists have criticized the English language for containing so many foreign words, most students of literature consider the size and variety of its vocabulary to be one of its great assets. But arguments of this kind, pro or con, miss the point that a language has a function as well as a history. Because it is the function of a language to convey thought and feeling as accurately as possible, the proper way to judge its quality is to see how well it keeps pace with expanding knowledge in an advanced civilization and serves the descriptive requirements of researchers in every field. Another important test is to examine its ability to meet the needs of great writers who in striving to express a thought most fully strain the resources of their language to the utmost.

The literature of the English language is the best evidence of its strength. From the earliest period of Middle English to the twentieth century, great writers have shown that it can be adapted to an almost infinite variety of styles without losing its essential form. As early as the fourteenth century the first great works written in Middle English, Chaucer's *Canterbury Tales* and Wycliff's translation of the Bible, revealed the beauty of the "new" language and the remarkable poetic effects inherent in combinations of French and Anglo-Saxon words.

The further expansion of the language through the adoption of Latin and Greek words occasionally led to absurd results—the result of excess, but it also strengthened English as a language for abstract thought in theology, philosophy, and criticism. The poets and playwrights of the sixteenth and seventeenth centuries (especially Shakespeare and Milton) wrote masterpieces that capitalized on the expressive possibilities of this expanded vocabulary.

In later periods the great writers from Dryden and Jonathan Swift to Hemingway and Robert Frost all contributed to the language by the same process of expansion, coupled with the aim of increasing flexibility. The writers of each generation act to preserve the unity and fixity, the clarity and forcefulness, and the sameness of the language without stifling its vitality and growth. The written language may be likened to a gyroscope that keeps its stability despite the continual vagaries of the spoken language. There is an intricate relationship between the literary tradition and the individual writer. The writer works within such a tradition while developing new powers of expression. This effort is the same as that of creators of music and the fine arts, except for the fact that language, unlike music or painting, is the much abused medium of daily communication.

It is misleading to talk about a language by itself, however, apart from the individuals who use it and apart from their experience. The real vitality of words is not something inherent in the sounds; it lies in their association with the actual life of individuals. Take a very simple example. When my oldest son was a little boy he used to come with us from New York to Far

Hills, New Jersey, to visit my mother on weekends. One day I was walking there with him in the fields. We had gone a little farther than Charlie thought safe with only his father at hand, so he told me we had better "go back to the country." For a moment I was stumped; then it dawned on me that for him the word *country* meant simply my mother's house. What could be more logical? When we said we were going to the country we always ended up there. This kind of semantic mix-up is not difficult to diagnose. The application of a certain word has been learned incorrectly; it must be relearned. But it was obviously far easier to clear up this misuse than it would have been to give a boy a clear notion of "the country" if he had never been out of the city. Experience underlies language.

Now let me turn to the likelihood that the problems of a literature and the deterioration of a language arise from precisely that same relationship of words to experience. To avoid misusing technical terms I may not fully understand, I should like to define my own informal terms for convenient use in this discussion. If we exclude logical terms like *and* or *not* and the like, every word has two different but related aspects: the first I call its *conventional application* and the second its *evocative capacity*.

The conventional application of a word in a given language is simply the set of all things or qualities of things with which we are taught to associate it. Dictionaries deal with the conventional applications of words, and wherever possible make explicit the rules or criteria determining to what things a given word applies. For example, one dictionary defines the word *table* as "an article of furniture consisting of a flat top resting on legs or on a pillar." Of course, the actual process of learning our own language and naming things correctly takes place largely without benefit of dictionaries. At the same time, this direct learning obviously requires a very sophisticated analysis of past and present experiences. This is all the more mysterious in that it is done unconsciously. In naming a familiar-looking object the word we have learned for it comes to mind, thanks to a process whereby the object has been judged to fall within the conventional application of the word. If the proper word does not come to mind, we are momentarily at a loss, because we cannot directly control the essential steps of this unconscious process.

Once a word has been associated with a specific experience it remains tied to the memory of that experience. Thus the word *table* is associated in our memories with an enormous number of objects of various sizes, shapes, and colors, as well as the variety of outward physical surroundings and inward emotional states in which they were perceived. Now these memories are the basis for the evocative capacity of the word. Evocation in this sense can be thought of as the reverse of the process of naming something. The evocative capacity of a word is the total of all the images, thoughts, and feelings it can produce in our consciousness. Obviously, the evocative power of a word is not absolute but relative. What a given word evokes in the minds of different people varies widely. The range depends, among other things, upon the education and life experience of each. Even for a single individual, what a word can elicit varies from time to time, and what a word evokes at any time differs as much from the word itself as a musical note differs from the piano key that makes it sound. But the analogy only goes so far: it would be an extraordinary piano if the same keys never produced exactly the same notes.

Words first attain evocative capacity through the simple naming of things—the firsthand experience during which each individual builds the fundamental vocabulary of his life. Most of it is acquired when we are still very young, and the vitality of our memories of childhood confirms the importance of what we learn then. Thus our first sight of a field scattered with wild strawberries (they were originally called "strewnberries" to convey this scattered aspect) will form in our memory the core of all that we subsequently associate with the name. This is also so with the naming of the flowers and birds and animals, seasons and stars and constellations, and all the furnishings of our childhood world. These are the elements, the foundations of our life-long response to words as such and to their use in literature. From this I infer that one of the most important contributions parents can make to the education of their children is the simple, continual naming of things. I concede that this may often require additional education for the parents.

A final point that I want to make about the evocative capacity of a word is that simple, familiar words like *table*, when taken alone, evoke only vague mental images. Since we cannot be conscious simultaneously of all our experiences of tables, our mind has little or no guidance in choosing any particular one. But if I narrow these experiences down to thinking, say, of the dining-room table in my home as a child, or of a work table at school, I find that much clearer memories enter my consciousness. This narrowing down describes one of the primary techniques of a good writer: he capitalizes on the evocative capacity of the words he uses by modifying or particularizing them just enough to prompt the reader's own memories in their fullest clarity.

Here as in virtually all forms of artistic creation the attainment of the balancing point is all-important: too many details, too much specificity, can abort the evocative process as surely as too little. Ernest Hemingway is one of the great stylists of fiction because he was incessantly preoccupied with the problem of evocative description. For him the solution lay in providing the key detail of an experience. The reader supplied the rest. For the writer, the trick is easier said than done. Hemingway tells, for example, of prodding his memory for one such detail in connection with the goring of a bullfighter. He finally realized that the detail he was searching for was the "unbearable clean whiteness" of the exposed thigh bone.

The opening paragraph of *A Farewell to Arms* is an excellent example of Hemingway at the height of his mastery of the evocative capacity of simple words:

> In the late summer of that year we lived in a house in a village that looked across the river and the plain to the mountains. In the bed of the river there were pebbles and boulders, dry and white in the sun, and the water was clear and swiftly moving and blue in the channels. Troops went by the house and down the road and the dust they raised powdered the leaves of the trees. The trunks of the trees too were dusty and the leaves fell early that year and we saw the troops marching along the road and the dust rising and leaves, stirred by the breeze, falling and the soldiers marching and afterward the road bare and white except for the leaves.

Indeed, from the time of Homer this has always been the storyteller's principal artistic objective: to use the evocative capacity of words to control the imagination of the listener or reader. Only in that way can the author induce the vivid and organized mental state characteristic of literature. For a poem or story is not just some kind of window through which we view what we have seen before. It is an authentic experience in itself, a special one created out of our own past experiences as "the word" evokes them.

Many books have so powerful an effect on us that we remember them with as much—sometimes even with greater —vividness than episodes in our own lives. That is the basis for the powerful social influence of literature—an influence the ancient Greeks sought to use in the education of the young. For generation after generation, the *Iliad* and the *Odyssey* constituted the fundamental common literary experience—one that shaped their religious imagination, their view of life, and the relevance of their drama and poetry.

Of comparable impact in their respective fields were the great masterpieces of Greek history and philosophy; and in later centuries the works of Virgil, Horace, Cicero, and Seneca; of Dante, Cervantes, Montaigne, Molière, and Shakespeare— not to mention the Bible, which has probably had the greatest impact of all. These works, and others in the same traditions, created common imaginative experiences shared by generations of readers and writers. From them there flowed into the English language thousands of names and expressions of great evocative capacity.

Consider in this respect how naturally John Keats makes use of the biblical heritage when he refers to "the sad heart of Ruth, when, sick for home, / She stood in tears amid the alien corn." Or William Wordsworth's use of the classical heritage in the lines "Have sight of Proteus rising from the sea; / Or hear old Triton blow his wreathèd horn." Or the mixture of references in Blake's stanza:

> The atoms of Democritus
> And Newton's particles of light
> Are sands upon the Red Sea shore,
> Where Israel's tents do shine so bright.

Is this reservoir of our language drying up, depending as it does on familiarity with great works of the past? I am almost certain it is—partly because of the virtual end of the classical tradition in literature and the atrophy of classical education, partly because of the decline in knowledge of the Bible, and partly because of the desultory and superficial character of so much of present-day education in the humanities. Our teaching of literature sometimes seems more an array of appetizers than a square meal. In particular literature today is often loaded down with complicated theories that obscure plain meanings and remove all pleasure in reading. An even more alarming development is that modern life robs many individuals of appreciating the evocative capacity of words related to nature.

When one considers the drastic urbanization and suburbanization of American life, one begins to understand how words may lose their power. Are we not creating with respect to the evocative capacity of language a nation of children that can only be called impoverished as compared with those of the past? I am afraid that we are. Right now the country is aroused and trying to tackle the complex problems of education. As parents and supporters of the public school, we must do all we can to restore the intimate knowledge of the natural world that was once acquired without special effort. Serious symptoms of spiritual malnutrition are already showing up in our vocabulary as it is shaped by twentieth-century technology and commercialism. Our thoughts and speeches are weighed down with such man-made objects as *station breaks*, *countdowns*, and *filter tips*. While we defoliate our landscape, we are indirectly defoliating our language, too. It is imperative that we rearrange our lives and the lives of our children so that words like *goldfinch* and *cardinal*, *goldenrod* and *honeysuckle*, *chipmunk* and *beaver*, *meadows* and *trout streams* will not be merely names in a book or exhibits in a museum but vividly memorable contacts with nature. Keats wrote that the "poetry of the earth is never dead." But it might as well have died if we become deaf to it.

As I said earlier, the firsthand experiences associated with a given word differ from one individual to another, and the passage of time also robs some words of their evocative capacity. Thus no exercise of historical imagination can fully restore to names like Caesar or Charlemagne the associations that they had for their contemporaries. In that sense, some words have become "bookish." What they connote depends more on what we have read than on what we have felt. Similarly, ignorance of geography limits the evocative capacity of words. Place names such as Rome or Cape Town or Hong Kong will be qualitatively different depending on whether one has visited these cities or merely read about them or seen pictures of them. These are all obvious examples of the inevitable "relativity" of words with respect to our experiences.

To young people growing up either in cities or in suburbs rapidly turning into cities, seeing the countryside face to face, as it were, is no longer part of life. Much of our land we see either from an altitude of forty thousand feet in the air or at a velocity of sixty miles an hour on the ground. We walk less and less, and though we talk we rarely converse, our leisure being spent mostly in sports or "entertainment." As these changes have taken place in our lives, thousands of words long precious to writers are steadily losing their evocative capacity. They will survive, if at all, as empty husks in dictionaries. Consider these two beautiful lines by George Santayana from his poem "The Poet's Testament": "I give back to the earth what the earth gave, / All to the furrow, nothing to the grave." For centuries poets could have used the word *furrow* with the certainty that it would evoke a vivid picture of plowing and planting in almost every reader's mind. The word *furrow* that is a corruption of the Roman word *porca* has had an unbroken continuity of association covering two thousand years. But what can the word evoke in the mind of someone who has to look it up in the dictionary?

Think of how filled Shakespeare's plays and poems are with the names of the common flowers of England: violets and primroses, daffodils and daisies and all the rest. We published in 1969 an unusually beautiful book entitled *Shakespeare's*

Flowers. The author, Jessica Kerr, explains in a most unusual way how familiar Shakespeare was with the flowers of the English countryside and gardens. He knew their forms, colors, perfumes, and their patterns of growth, as well as the traditional legends and beliefs associated with each flower. Rosemary and rue, violets and daffodils, oxlips and wild thyme are only a few of the names in Shakespeare's cast of floral characters. He used these names and myths sometimes as the basis for figures of speech relating to human traits, sometimes as a means of creating atmosphere through a verbal picture. Shakespeare could be confident that his audience could follow his meaning.

The gifted Scribner writer Loren Eiseley had a fascination with the macabre aspects of nature and was able to meld scenes of the natural world into his writings. For example, Eiseley once recounted how the sphinx larvae would capture bees and insects, ensnare the creatures underground where they were immobilized with poison, and then gradually have the creatures eaten alive by their brood. Eiseley likened the scene in the sphinx lair to that of a Roman prison.

It is not that our modern words—*wavelength* and *sound barrier, data base* and *splashdown*—do not have their own evocative capacity; it is simply that they do not begin to restore what we have lost in our break with nature. Nor do they serve literature to any extent. We cannot afford to lose contact with our earth in this way. Many of us have been taught to depreciate the work of the Romantic poets, but their thoughts and feelings about nature may in the long run turn out to have been wiser than our own. Wordsworth deplored that we see little in nature that is ours, but what could he have said to a generation that sees little of nature at all?

I believe, moreover, that nature has given us the fundamental models of beauty. The reason for this linkage lies in the dual aspect of our sense of beauty. For example when we look at a flower, let us say a common daisy, one part of our mind perceives the form of the flower pattern we see in all of them and which we can express geometrically. At the same time, another part of our mind responds to the spontaneous vitality of the flower, which asserts itself against that form in every petal.

Analogous duality between form and spontaneity can be seen in all the arts from music to painting. It is significant that in a period when many artists have turned away from nature for inspiration we find existing side by side two virtually contradictory schools of contemporary painting: one exploring form without spontaneity and the other spontaneity without form. Such developments are indirectly related to the impoverishment of our language, to which the uprootedness of contemporary life contributes.

This brings me to the end of my attempt to answer the question of whether our language is deteriorating. I believe it is, insofar as whole families of words have lost their evocative capacity through changes in our education and way of life. In arguing for the preservation of the English language it is important to prevent any misunderstandings as to what is intended. Preserving the language does not mean trying to revive words that have become obsolete as the result of changes in the life of the nation. Such words—for example, the vocabulary of horse-shoeing—are preserved in dictionaries but have naturally fallen out of general use. Nor does language conservation mean refusing to admit new words that have been coined to cover new items in the life of the nation—for example, the language of aviation. But writers who wish to communicate effectively are slow to use current jargon or slang; they know from experience how soon such words become meaningless.

The real aim of preserving a language is to try to prevent the loss of those words or constructions that have contributed to its clarity and expressiveness. Critics who deplore the misuse of an important word are not simply motivated by snobbery or useless regard for "good form." Their real concern is whether the language is losing its capacity to express important ideas and distinguish between them.

Preserving the language is also desirable if one wishes to maintain the continuity of an intellectual, political, and social tradition. Educated readers today need special training before they can go back six centuries in time to read the poetry of Chaucer. They can read Shakespeare with comparatively little assistance other than to explicate the obsolete words or those that have changed meaning. From the eighteenth century on, the literature is easily accessible.

In our museums and concert halls we delight in the artistic creations of earlier centuries. It would be an unconscionable loss if our language changed so much that the great works in the literary canon became unreadable. And that would not be the only loss. There are also the great books in English on science, social philosophy, political thought, travel, religion, and ethics, which are the sources of many of our ideas and institutions. If linguistic change is rapid and heedless, these works, too, will soon be as inaccessible as if they had been written in Latin or Greek—closed books to all but scholars.

I should like to venture a word about the future on this point, but the complexity of the issue is daunting. If our language and literature reflect the nature of our common experiences, then any predictions about them necessarily involve assumptions about broader historical trends: in religion, in city life, in education, in the whole spirit of our society. I do have a hunch, although it is very scantily clothed in evidence, that we may now be in the very early stages of what will be considered a major "Romantic revival," similar to the one that swept Europe in the early nineteenth century. There are several clues for this: the spiritual dissatisfaction of young people; growing anti-intellectualism; the crusading zeal of conservationists, who include so many men and women from our scientific community; and, finally, the obvious yearning of families for contact with nature, as revealed by the popularity of camping trips and vacation homes in the country.

If this "Romantic revival" is indeed taking place, it will be bound to affect our language in interesting ways and change our literary fashions, too. It is something that I, for one, am hoping to see blossom and bear fruit.

The Heuristic
Power of Writing

❧

In a little book of 1911 entitled *An Introduction to Mathematics*, the English philosopher and scientist Alfred North Whitehead pointed out that "civilization advances by extending the number of important operations we can perform without thinking about them." However strange Whitehead's idea may seem to those who believe that the daily life of modern man is filled with feats of the mind, it is a familiar truth to students of intellectual history. We have advanced beyond our primitive ancestors because of the techniques we have been taught rather than because of any superiority of brains; and with every advance of civilization we become even more dependent on the achievements of the past.

A schoolchild with modest proficiency in the three R's—the foundation of all formal education—has inherited techniques that are of enormous efficiency compared with the efforts of a culture without an alphabet or a number system. He is able, virtually without thinking, to read a written word, transcribe a spoken word, and do simple arithmetic—all of this being of no particular credit to him but to people of the past.

Many other benefits of civilization come from transforming what were once difficult operations into mechanical ones that can be taught to children. These simplifications eliminate a great deal of mental drudgery and free the mind to tackle other tasks. But before one becomes unduly optimistic about the ultimate future of a civilization in which the need for thinking is continually reduced, it would be well to consider some of the difficulties that arise along the way as the very result of the simplifying techniques.

First, there is the danger that an operation that can be performed without thinking will be learned without understanding. This pedagogical difficulty besets teachers in every field. Various attempts to teach reading without phonics have shown the fallacy of trying to make such a skill a mechanical one before it has been adequately understood. Every student should be helped to grasp the idea behind what he is learning. Otherwise it will seem to the student that he or she is being taught something mysterious, and the pupil's performance will be hampered—sometimes permanently—by lack of insight and confidence.

Furthermore, it is a mistake to suppose that to free the mind from having to think about daily tasks will result in higher levels of cerebration. While some minds may look for new fields to conquer, it is likely, judging from present trends, that many more minds will lapse into intellectual apathy and indifference to civilization itself.

The prospect of such an intellectual decline does not alarm those who believe in the unlimited progress of technology. Computers have made contributions so extraordinary to industry and scientific research that, in the opinion of enthusiasts, these "thinking machines" may shortly match all the powers of the human mind and initially remove the need for schools and colleges. This prophecy, however, overlooks the important fact that a computer, like its primitive counterpart the adding machine, can perform only operations that do not require thought. A human mind must think through a complex problem—step by step—before a computer can be programmed to solve it. Far from eliminating the necessity of thinking, computers often require of professionals in any field creative imagination of a high order. To impute to the machine the intelligence of its user is sheer superstition.

As civilization advances, the rapidity of change in all aspects of life raises innumerable problems that call for clear thinking. In religion, politics, and economics, as well as in the arts and sciences, the best thought of the best minds will always be needed to resolve the fundamental uncertainties that are bound to arise.

Thinking is hard work. It involves parts of one's mind that are not directly subject to the will, and that fact in itself weakens one's confidence. Racking the brain over a problem is fatiguing and painful. The great figures in the life of the mind have often shown heroic endurance in their pursuit of enlightenment. And when one looks for the forces that motivated them, one is baffled. Intellectual curiosity, love of learning, delight in beauty, and yearning for understanding are all characteristics of creative minds; why these traits predominate in some minds remains a mystery.

This being so, no single aim of educational research can be more important than to find better ways to stimulate in young minds this type of curiosity and intellectual ambition. It so happens that learning to write often provides that stimulus, for not only is writing an indispensable practical skill, but written composition is also an art closely related to the growth of the intellect. The very act of writing makes for the creation and clarification of thought. One may call this psychological effect of writing its "heuristic power." I have searched for a simpler word than "heuristic" but have been unable to find one that seems to me to do justice to the way in which the process of writing fosters intellectual bravery and originality.

Before I examine how writing has widened the scope of the creative imagination, a few, possibly obvious, observations about its origins as a practical invention should be made. Writing is subordinate to speech. To refer to the "written word" suggests that written records were made in various civilizations only after elaborate systems of linguistic expression had already been well developed, together with the corresponding patterns of thought. Man spoke and thought in a language before he learned to write.

It was natural therefore that written expression should have been assimilated to an already existing system of communication. This assimilation was awkward and cumbersome in its early stages, but in Western civilization at least, the correspondence between the written and the spoken word became increasingly close. Largely through the invention of simple alphabets based on sounds, writing eventually became a kind of material speech.

What I have just described is familiar but by no means trivial. Recalling the historical evolution of writing helps to explain why what we read and write is as immediately compatible with our thought processes as what we hear and say. And it is this well-developed affinity between writing and thinking that has made writing such an extraordinarily powerful intellectual implement. Writing, in short, is a train of thought made visible and arrested in time. One shapes and modifies thought by editing its written expression. This, in turn, might be described as externalizing the process of thinking.

An important invention like writing often requires a very long time to develop, advancing by fits and starts. Even after the invention of writing, the growth of a diversified written literature fulfilling the unique potential of written composition needed far more time and far more innovation than we generally suppose. To cite but one thing, the inconvenience of most early writing materials presented many obstacles to their extensive—let alone universal—use.

One may also wonder if the existence in many preliterate civilizations of rich and ancient oral traditions may not also have held up the development of written works. The first uses of writing appear to have been limited: to ensure the permanence of very specific textual records—religious formulas, political decrees, and catalogs of royal achievements and possessions. On a more mundane level, one also finds written inventories of goods and records of business agreements. Coexisting with these matters that were given the special treatment of writing were oral repertories of poetry, legends, and liturgies. These were never written down for the simple reason that it did not seem necessary to do so.

It would be next to impossible to untangle all the strands in the origins of a written literary tradition within a given civilization. Even for ancient Greece, where the flowering of literature was so impressive, the evolution is not entirely clear; many important links have been lost. But some generalizations can be safely made.

As early as the eighth century B.C. the Greeks appear to have made relatively sophisticated efforts to gather together material from their oral tradition and to give this material artistic unity. The most important undertaking of this kind was the composition of the two Homeric epics. How this was done or when or by whom cannot be established. Nor is it clear to what extent, if any, these two poems as we know them were set down in writing. But it is certain that they embody a large amount derived from the oral tradition.

Much of the earliest Greek literature in writing may well have been simply compilations from this source. By then it was only a matter of a few generations before the Greeks were taking full advantage of the art of writing. Many of their greatest thinkers were also teachers, a fact that spurred them to find ways in which otherwise complicated fields of knowledge could be comprehended clearly and easily. This effort can be seen in the fragments we have of pre-Socratic thought. It is plain that written composition would have helped to attain these goals of clarity and simplicity. Obviously a written draft makes it easy to produce a work of some length in which the various parts may have to be reviewed or modified in the course of composition. It seems likely that the Greeks were the first nation to discover how well the act of writing serves to prompt and guide the articulation of thought—the familiar interaction between clear writing and clear thinking. Part of the Greeks' intellectual vigor may have arisen from the freshness of their discovery of that power inherent in writing.

The transition from a predominantly oral to a predominantly written literary tradition had other consequences beyond a direct contribution to intellectual creativity. The permanence of writing was bound to affect the public role of the individual author, as well as his own view of his work. In preliterate society a storyteller-poet performed his works for the benefit of face-to-face audiences. In our own time this still holds true with the live performances of actors, musicians, lecturers, and classroom teachers. The full impact of modern recording techniques has not been felt in these activities.

Once written literature became well established, ancient authors associated the ways in which written versions of their works extended their influence beyond that of the spoken word. A writer's thought and style could survive his death. This idea is expressed in the triumphant words of the Roman poet Horace: "I have built a monument more enduring than bronze . . . not all of me will die."

To us it seems natural that a writer should be given great incentives to exhibit an individual literary identity through publication. He could now individualize his work in various ways—through technical virtuosity, by putting fresh vigor into old literary genres, by developing new forms, and above all by cultivating a characteristic style of his own. He would endeavor to glean fresh ideas and material from the experiences of his life. These make for a personalizing of literature characteristic of the written tradition. For example, this revelation of the author's personality helps to explain the striking difference in style between Homer's *Iliad* and Virgil's *Aeneid*, a difference that makes Virgil seem far closer to our own times than to Homer's.

Some critics find in the unselfconsciousness and impersonality of folk literature virtues not existing in more sophisticated written traditions. Yet a writer's striving for identity has often been the mainspring of his creativity. Reinforced by the psychological effects of the act of writing, this striving has been a cultural force of enormous importance. An interesting case of a writer's self-discovery as the result of his writing is that of the sixteenth-century French essayist Montaigne. Like many educated men of his time, Montaigne was deeply influenced by the authors, and especially the moral philosophers, of the ancient world. But in his case this enthusiasm took a creative turn, for upon his retirement from the Parlement (the law courts) of Bordeaux he began to try his hand at composing little philosophical pieces of history, with emphasis on aspects of human behavior.

As Montaigne viewed this literary enterprise, he was essentially testing the validity of his own ideas by comparing them with those of ancient writers. He called these compositions *essais* to convey the tentative, experimental aspect of what he was doing. As a consequence of his method, many of his earlier essays were quite bookish and derivative, and not merely because they were laced with quotations from Seneca and Plutarch and other Roman and Greek writers. But as he went on he became more self-confident and intellectually independent, coming more and more to express original ideas and to document these by means of interesting examples drawn from his life and times. He developed a characteristic style and began to speak with what was clearly his own voice. His writing has led him to authentic creation. Indeed, this was Montaigne's view of his literary career. He spoke of a book being cosubstantial with its author. As he put it very simply, "I have no more made my book than my book has made me."

The history of literature provides many other examples of the way in which writing nurtures the writer and sends the author on the journey to self-discovery. Sometimes these effects have been interpreted superficially as evidence of the writer's having done no more than acquire a special skill through practice, much as he might have learned shorthand or typing. But what is involved in literary creation is surely something far deeper. Writing triggers thoughts that otherwise arise only rarely in the everyday life of the mind. This may be the result of a particular form of concentration, but, whatever the psychological explanation, the process yields insights and ideas of the greatest value—all of which testify to what I have called the heuristic power of writing.

As I see it, the writer is continually harvesting his or her own mind and memories, acquiring a depth of self-knowledge otherwise unattainable. This is the joy-inducing aspect of writing for those who discover in what they have written something they were not aware they knew. This same effort is the anguish-inducing aspect for those who find themselves repeat-edly frustrated by the fact that this potential for discovery is only partly subject to their will. As a book publisher, I have observed dramatic manifestations of both emotions, often in the same person.

Given the extent to which good writing *is* subject to the individual will, I am saddened when I see how often too little thought is devoted to this endeavor. Every month at least a hundred manuscripts are submitted to publishers such as Scribners. They come either from literary agents or from hopeful authors acting on their own behalf, or from someone who has found an ancestor's memoirs in the attic. Each is considered in an examination that ranges from a brief but sufficient screening to a series of readings by different persons.

It is dismaying to see how few of these unsolicited works have the slightest chance of getting published. A fair number of the manuscripts are downright crazy in one way or another; the majority are appallingly deficient in even the most elementary writing skills. I sometimes wonder if our experience in that respect is shared by music publishers and play producers. How is it possible that so many aspiring writers should know so little about writing? It is easy to speak of elementary writing skills, but what does the phrase mean? It may be worth outlining what our editors look for in a manuscript. The first principle—a matter of overriding importance—is that the writer must be able to keep the reader continually in mind. The written word, like the spoken word on which it is based, is a means of communication, and there are two sides to communication. As with the telephone, there is a transmitter and a receiver. The person doing the talking, the person writing, must make sure that his or her ideas are capable of getting across to the listener or reader.

This sounds so obvious that it should go without saying. But from the number of hopelessly flawed works submitted to us

every week, what is much more obvious is that this is not obvious enough. Aspiring writers seem to forget the reader altogether as they set their thoughts down on paper. They are writing on water if their thoughts do not enter the reader's mind
surely and accurately. So our first major responsibility is to
make sure that the reader is not forgotten. Nearly all the corrections and suggestions we make to authors are to improve
the process of communication they have neglected. Because
the statement of a given idea or event is perfectly clear to the
author, this is no guarantee that the writer has achieved the
corresponding degree of clarity in the reader's mind.
Beginning writers whose works have been read only by well-
wishers in the family seem especially prone to this type of
blindness.

This first principle explains why many people can write rea-
sonably effective letters but go to pieces when they tackle the
essay or short story. The nature of letter writing compels them
to keep the other person in mind. It is not surprising that one
of the earliest English novelists, Samuel Richardson, wrote his
Clarissa in the form of letters—he was a professional letter
writer for his illiterate neighbors. A good many other writers
since Richardson, including Ring Lardner, have used the letter
form of story-telling. In the early 1980s Scribners awarded the
Maxwell Perkins Prize for a first novel to a young woman
named Margaret Mitchell Dukore who used this same technique. Writing a series of letters to tell a short story would be a
useful exercise for many inexperienced writers. When a writer
remains focused on the reader as a lecturer does on the audience in order to keep it awake, the result is manifest. Part of
the magic of Lewis Carroll's *Alice in Wonderland* is due to the
fact that he was writing it for one little girl. Many nineteenth-
century writers used the conceit of addressing the "dear reader." The device is old-fashioned, but the underlying idea is still

good. Who knows? It may have helped those authors to write so as to be read.

An equally general principle is that the reader one is addressing in a given work must shape that work's style and stance. When Albert Einstein wrote his first paper on relativity for a German scientific journal, his ideas and arguments were couched in a language different from that which he used later when he attempted to explain his theory to the so-called general reader. Einstein was a very able writer, and the idea of the *relativity* of a writer's style did not escape him.

As everybody knows, virtually all the adult books sold in bookstores or circulated by libraries are composed with the hope of reaching a national audience. Of this audience, the average author rarely gets to meet more than a handful. Most writers lack the advantage that ancient storytellers and bards enjoyed—that of seeing the audience sitting in front of them and being able to gauge the success of their presentation. All that the modern writers can assume of their readers is a reasonable command of the language. If a writer expects too much or too little, he or she is in trouble. Most writers—usually with some help from their editors—manage to avoid these extremes. The success of *Finnegans Wake* on the one hand and of *Jonathan Livingston Seagull* on the other suggests that the range of acceptability is broad indeed.

Turning to the writer, it is plain that when writers choose to ignore the needs of their readers and indulge in the vacuous jargon or long-winded abstractions that have been called "nonsense on stilts" writing will become not only futile for them but also harmful to their educations: writing will widen the gap between what they know and what they profess to know. Obscure writing is not exceptional: celebrated authorities have been guilty of it, touted critics today set a very poor example, and scholarly journals are not above reproach. What is even more deplorable, some books each year become fashionable despite their impenetrability—or because of it.

Although criticism gives much attention to style, I think it is a mistake for aspiring writers to worry about it. If you concentrate on whether you are making yourself understood—which of course will influence your choice of words, the structure of your sentences, and the organization of your whole work—your style will take care of itself. Trying to make your words or sentences "stylish" is the surest way to sound false, affected. Think of your sentences as bricks in a building. No architect attempts to put style into each brick. His chief concern is the effect of the building as a whole.

In a novel, which is a kind of building on paper, the effect of the whole is also a function of clarity, of visibility. I will explore later the use of significant detail to create the impression of vividly seeing. But novels and plays also depend for their memorableness on characterization. Time and again, as I think, their success hinges on what you could call one obsessive character—a man or woman driven toward some end either for good or evil. When I started making a list of literature's truly memorable leading characters, I soon saw obsession at work and realized at the same time that these driven characters are needed to carry the plot forward. Anna Karenina and Madame Bovary give up their marriage and standing in society, as does Proust's Charles Swann, as a result of being obsessed with love. Don Quixote is so obsessed with his chivalric ideal to tilt with windmills and attack sheep. Balzac's Cousine Bette has a hatred for her family so strong that she finds a way to destroy them despite her complete paralysis using only her eyes.

In the character of the despicable Culp, Charles Dickens has created one of the most terrifying of villains. Beside him Shakespeare's Iago looks like a Salvation Army colonel. One of

Dickens's great gifts is his ability to conjure up an almost inexhaustible company of colorful characters: dishonest lawyers, grog-drinking clerics, a nameless waiter seen in passing—even a Shetland pony, Whisker, who belongs in every pantheon of animal characters. Everything Dickens touched turned to life, and although he assails our hearts in ways that are not fashionable today, it is unjust to forget the cruel sufferings of the poor and the weak of his time. Dickens's was a powerful voice for compassion and reform that, in Aleksandr Solzhenitsyn's phrase, made him "a second government" in Victorian England.

Modern "obsessionals" include Popeye in William Faulkner's *Sanctuary*, Captain Ahab in *Moby-Dick*, and the father in *The Winslow Boy*, who almost destroys his son in trying to exonerate him from an old theft of five shillings. Finally, there is the marvelous example in *Gone With the Wind* of Scarlett O'Hara and Rhett Butler. It was Rhett all the women fell for, not Ashley.

Why are we so fascinated by powerful personalities, regardless of their evil? Is it not that we admire—perhaps envy—their single-mindedness, ruthlessness, fearlessness of consequences? How rare it is to find such persons in our own lives! We overlook their self-destruction because they give us the opportunity, at least for a short time, to identify ourselves with their power to will, to act, to change others' lives and their own.

In the depiction of characters larger than life, writers must exercise the greatest art in the choice not only of traits but of words. As Mark Twain put it, "The difference between the right word and the almost right word is the difference between lightning and the lightning bug."

And words matter not merely when used literally but also, and especially, when used to create figures, similes, and metaphors. Several years ago I reread Marcel Proust's *Remem-*

brance of Things Past, and I began to notice how frequently Proust made use of scientific facts for his images. The novel contains over two hundred such references, which I later cataloged in the *Proceedings of the American Philosophical Society*. As one ponders them, it becomes clear that Proust's aim was not in the least didactic; it was to make the passages vivid by shocking the reader through unexpected comparison.

Proust presumes that the reader will generally be familiar enough with science to understand the images. For example, when one reads of the young boy at Combray seeing the tadpoles coalesce around bread crumbs as though they were crystals in solution, one remembers that simile forever. Elsewhere, Proust writes, "[There] came to us, faint, horizontal, but dense and metallic still, echoes of the bells of Saint-Hilaire, which had not melted into the air they had traversed for so long, and, ribbed by the successive palpitation of all their sound-waves, throbbed as they grazed the flowers at our feet." Through his choice of words and allusion to science, Proust shows us scenes or actions that are familiar enough but are transfigured into new visions of reality. The reader is incited to perceive the juxtaposed touches exactly as in an Impressionist painting.

If writing is to be kept as clear as possible, the writer must continually study the logic, the order, the coherence of what he or she wishes to convey. Ideas are like suitcases—hard to pick up unless one uses the handle. It is the writer's task to provide that handle for the reader. In striving for clarity and simplicity, you will eliminate everything in your writing that may seem hazy or superfluous; it will force you to dig deeper into your mind so as to reach the logic of your subject, while you find a point of view from which it will appear in its greatest simplicity. At the same time you will be scanning the mind of the reader so as to anticipate the places where he may lose the thread of what you are saying. When you become proficient in making your words fit both the logic of the subject and the psychology of the reader, you will have acquired the essential attributes of a great teacher. The requirements of good writing will have taught you how to tell things to others—that is, to be a teacher yourself.

Throughout the history of the novel, from Cervantes to Solzhenitsyn, what writers have striven for is something more—something other—than perfect style as an end in itself. They have sought to fashion a form that would convey visions of life that possess the impact of life itself. That is why I do not cheer when someone speaks of a book as being a "reading experience." To my way of thinking, reading a book may or may not be *an experience*.

In 1980 the U.S. Post Office issued a new stamp lauding the virtues of letter writing and asked me to write something for the First Day Cover. What I said was: "There is a mystery—even a paradox—surrounding the power of writing. Perhaps one is made more aware of the mind and spirit of the writer when one has nothing before one but his or her very words. Whatever the explanation, all of us share the experience."

Whoever becomes a writer to any degree has come to grips consciously and steadily with words as such, with the spirit and genius of his or her mother tongue. From then on, what the author writes and what he or she reads will interact, each enhancing the degree of the writer's mastery. But there is more to the joint addiction than power and excitement. Devotees of the word stress its value in preserving and disseminating ideas, but too little has been said about its role in the creation of new ideas.

Young people these days often talk of "expanding" their consciousness. It is not altogether clear what they mean by that, but they go in for drugs or meditation to carry out that purpose. They regularly overlook one of the best means—learning to write. Setting fragments of one's consciousness on paper and shaping them into thought by revision is an "expanding" discipline; it has given joy and heightened the sense of life for writers. Authors who read their finished work discover with pleasure and surprise that they have extracted from their minds ideas, memories, and wisdom that they had not suspected they possessed. Writing exploits resources of heart and mind that everyday life leaves dormant. The call on faculties unused is what artists of every sort mean by the reality of "inspiration"— namely, the spontaneous occurrence of ideas all unsought, sometimes (for writers) the wording of whole passages, risen from an unconscious.

Writing also reshapes the mind, trains it to develop special habits. Authors are curious about everything they see and hear. Who knows what may be grist for their mill? In any one experience the writer will notice details that escape the casual observer. Hark back to my describing Hemingway as a young man in Paris struggling to perfect himself as a writer and setting himself the task of writing "one true sentence." For him and others, the best style is a clear glass through which the reader simply sees. One might call this principle of writing the theory of "immediacy."

In view of the importance of writers and writing in a nation's culture, it seems appropriate to ask certain questions. For example, How successfully are our schools teaching composition? I am not thinking now only about students who may have a special talent, but about the whole college-bound generation. Exercises in writing will help very little in learning to think until one has attained minimum competence in putting words together coherently. Next, To what extent do our colleges require the prior attainment of this level of writing competence?

Perhaps the task of teaching writing is more difficult today, when our society has devised so many substitutes for the written word. Telephone calls substitute for letters, and unrehearsed panel discussions for lectures. Keeping a diary is nearly obsolete, although in the past the habit was a valuable aid to professional writers. Radio and television are relentlessly taking over the core function of newspapers and magazines. Filmmaking is already beginning to take the place of writing as a means of self-expression. Through sheer disuse we may eventually reach the point where normal writing ability will be as rare among college graduates as is proficiency in higher mathematics. It may not be a lost art but a specialized one, practiced only by scholars—and few of them at that. The Muses will have become handmaidens of Minerva alone.

Though I have cited great authors as examples, it should not be thought that writing has no value unless published commercially. Just as many people derive great pleasure from playing a musical instrument without ever performing in Carnegie Hall, and many people enjoy painting and drawing without having their pieces hung in the Louvre, so writing can profit the private devotee. The arts can and ought to be practiced for their own sake—or, rather, for *our* sake, the sake of self-cultivation and spiritual enrichment.

Let me add one more observation before leaving the topic of self-education through writing. As a student of the history of science I have read a great deal of famous scientists' works, technical and nontechnical, and I have been struck by how extraordinarily literate most of these men and women were— fully as eloquent and as imaginative as humanists. Is this the result of their scientific prowess, or is it part of their scientific creativity attributable to the liberal education in which they learned to write well? The latter seems more likely.

I have mentioned the largely mechanical substitutes for writing that modern society now prefers. I could also list the difficulties that these same devices create for the aspiring writer: getting published, starting out as a cub reporter, finding an outlet for fiction in magazines—all these traditional means of breaking into the circle of writers with a capital W are less and less available. To one part of the population, film and television represent progress, but I remain deeply skeptical. I doubt that any other form of communication can ever take the place of writing as the proper medium of the intellect. However beset or confined, reading and writing are now and will continue to be the essential arts of the life of the mind. Indeed, they *are* the life of the mind. I must therefore regard all machine-born developments with mingled curiosity, apprehension, and hope.

Books and the
Life of the Mind

☙

In the 1970s at a publishers' luncheon club in New York the guest speaker, a man who had played a major role in developing new programs for commercial television, took as his subject "The Wired Society and the Hardcover Book." It was, of course, a matter of some importance to us publishers to find out whether in the future there would still be a place for the book—with or without wires.

The speaker began by predicting that very soon cable television would greatly expand as the result of new technology. In time, every home would have access to dozens—perhaps hundreds—of separate cable channels. Homebodies would then have, literally at their fingertips, a seemingly unlimited amount of entertainment and information, ranging from Archie Bunker to Hamlet, from crocheting to quantum theory. All this audiovisual material would be pumped into the house like electricity, water, and gas. Perhaps it would be similarly metered.

Our speaker went on to assure us that writers and publishers need not fear such a development. Indeed, they should consider themselves very fortunate as the proprietors of so much of the literary material that will be used for broadcast and piped—or cabled—into the house. As he put it, "The writers will be providing the necessary software." I suppose that we should always hope for the best when we hear such predictions, but judging from the cultural achievements of cable television so far, I am not very hopeful about the future of literature in a wired society.

At the same time, though, I think it is possible that in this further extension of television the merit of books and the efficiency of the written word will become more, rather than less, apparent. It may well be that the wired society will blow a fuse and have a blackout—perhaps in its finances or elsewhere, say, in its appeal as information and entertainment. So before one decides to recycle one's books and burn the bookcases and have another outside hole drilled into the basement, it would be well to take a good look at books taken by themselves, apart from the material they may provide for cable television.

Few human powers are so apparently simple or so profoundly important to the life of the mind as reading and writing. We take them for granted, but our society runs a serious risk when it toys with audiovisual means as a substitute for literacy. To continue our survey of language and the life of the mind, the invention of signs for writing took place much later than man's ability to speak intelligibly. But we know from cave paintings that men of the Old Stone Age had learned to record an event pictorially. If each object represented already had been given an equivalent word, we may see the germ of writing in those prehistoric pictures. Certainly the earliest forms of writing in the ancient Mediterranean kingdoms of Egypt, Mesopotamia, and Crete were based on little pictures of things, also denoted by words.

In the course of time some of those Egyptian pictograms, or hieroglyphs, came to be associated with the sound of the first syllables of the spoken words they represented. A combination of these special symbols or "phonograms" could therefore be used to represent other words on the basis of the sounds, rather than on the meanings. That was a tremendous innovation. By abstracting and simplifying, the phonograms of Egyptian writing led to the invention of letters, which formed alphabets, including the one our children learn—or ought to learn—in school. It could be argued that the alphabet is the most important invention in history. A picture is *no longer* worth a thousand words. It is alphabetical spelling that makes it relatively easy to master the art of reading and writing. This is the fundamental fact that is culpably ignored when we teach beginners by the "look and say" method instead of by the method of phonics.

When we appreciate this fact in the context of modern society—that is, when we put a proper value on the written and readable word—we are talking about books. It was not until after the vast conquests of Alexander the Great, in the Hellenistic Age, that books began to play a primary role in the life of the mind. By then it was no longer possible to absorb by memory, or transmit by word of mouth, the huge amounts of literature of all kinds that had been produced as the result of close contacts among many alien civilizations. The Hellenistic cities of Pergamum and Alexandria became centers of a cosmopolitan civilization, basically Greek. From Pergamum we get the word *parchment*, a substitute for papyrus in bookmaking; and from Byblos, another bookmaking town, we derive *Bible, bibliography*, and related terms. Great libraries (*bibliothekai*) were established in many cities, some with resident faculties of scholars, literary critics, and scientists.

These institutions continued to flourish under Roman domination. The works of the great Latin writers of the Augustan Age—including Horace and Virgil—were clearly inspired by Hellenistic traditions. And of course it was through Roman copies that the texts of the Greek classics were transmitted to the modern world. Indeed, making copies of the works of Greek and Roman writers was a flourishing trade throughout the then-known Western world. Since this labor had to be done painstakingly by hand, these "publishers" hit upon the time-saving expedient of having one person read aloud to a team of several dozen copyists. It was also the Romans who developed the book in its present form—that is, a collection of pages sewn together on one edge and having text on both sides of each page. It was a great improvement over the cumbersome papyrus rolls, and a "codex" could contain much longer texts, in some cases as long as the entire Bible.

After the decline of Rome and the breakup of its empire, the great libraries were sacked and destroyed. If the Christian monastic orders had not been filled by men committed to books and reading, the sequence of hand-copied texts would have been broken and only a trickle of classical literature could have flowed into the modern world. It is amusing to think of a pious monk industriously making copies of pagan works that must have seemed to him nothing short of scandalous. One hopes that in the feverishly erotic works of Catullus or Ovid some of the hidden meanings escaped him.

In the High Middle Ages the great Scholastic theologians such as Thomas Aquinas reinterpreted the works of Greek philosophy in the light of Christian doctrine and in doing so helped to keep unbroken the chain of copying that reaches back sixteen hundred years to Plato and Aristotle. But the time was not ripe for intellectuals to accept the worldview of classi-

cal authors as that is now understood. Only in the late fourteenth century did economic and social conditions in the large
towns of western Europe foster a consuming interest in classical culture. In that period the ancient books copied and
recopied over the centuries constituted a kind of time capsule
newly opened for study and enjoyment. The demand for further copies was so great that the invention of printing with
movable type seems almost inevitable.

This Renaissance in Italy was the beginning of a neoclassical
cultural tradition that has influenced nearly every aspect of
modern European civilization. We can compare its impact on
the Western world to the impact of Greek culture on the
Romans, centuries earlier, but this time it was done almost
entirely by and through books. To the artists of the Renaissance
the ancient masterpieces provided not only stunning models to
follow but also an enticing vision of new worlds to conquer by
their own genius.

The rediscovered ancients were similarly challenging and
inspiring for historians and philosophers. The literature of the
Greeks and Romans put the moderns in direct contact with
what appeared to be a wiser civilization. In the lovely phrase of
W. H. Auden, it became possible for then-new humanists "to
break bread with the past."

This revelation of the classical authors to their Renaissance
readers is probably the most impressive example of the role of
books in the life of the mind. It is all the more impressive when
one considers that only a fraction of the corpus of ancient literature survived into modern times by escaping the repeated
sacking and pillaging and burning of the homes and the
libraries that had housed them. The sum total of surviving
major works is numbered only in the hundreds. The Loeb
Classical Library, which reproduces these books in translation,

can be shelved in a bookcase of modest size, and it is no extraordinary feat for anyone to read them all. One is amazed at the thought of so small a reading list having so powerful and pervasive an influence. But it gave an extraordinary cultural impetus to Western civilization when generation after generation of educated men and women shared those books as a common intellectual experience. "The classics" in the curriculum and outside afforded a perspective of some two thousand years over the whole range of human achievement.

In very recent times, under the pressure of science and social science, Greek and Latin were progressively ousted from the schools and are no longer required for admission to universities. This has created a radical break in our cultural tradition. I shall not compare it to the Fall of Rome, but the disadvantages resulting from the decline in classical studies have been manifest. The great reading list of ancient authors is no longer the common experience of every educated man and woman. The two testaments of the Bible have suffered a similar fate. This great gap, this double loss, creates a more serious situation than is admitted by the intrepid innovators in American education and promoters of wired entertainment. As our daily lives become more complex and as the proliferation of specialties in all fields of knowledge limit our range within the life of the mind, it is all the more important that we should share a significant body of ideas and imaginative experiences. They not only form a bond similar to any other common background, but they also act as a means of communication with one another. There is such a thing as a common language *of ideas*, and it comes from reading the same books.

Recognizing the value of reading to civilization at large, most countries today have made their educational goal consist of steadily increasing the number of people able to read and write. The production of books in cheap editions has brought a wide choice within the means of most people—at least in the so-called developed countries—and school and free public libraries have enlarged their opportunities to read.

For all these reasons we might think of ourselves as living in a predominantly literate society, but this is by no means the case. In a curious way, the same progress in science and technology that has contributed to the spread of the written word has also produced a series of inventions that have introduced competing types of communication and entertainment that are nonliterate and, most lately, nonverbal.

The ubiquitous telephone has reduced letter writing to the minimum even for business purposes. The telephone was the logical sequel to the telegraph, by which Morse enabled people to transmit verbal messages very rapidly through sequences of electrical impulses along a wire. His code converted the letters of the alphabet into the familiar dots and dashes that bear his name. Next, Alexander Graham Bell's telephone converted the sound waves of the user's voice to produce a series of electrical impulses that were instantly reconverted into sound waves at the other end of the line. Somewhat later, Edison, who was trying to improve on the telephone voice box, saw in a flash of inspiration the possibility of letting the sound waves of the human voice inscribe themselves mechanically on some material as a moving soundtrack—in his first machine a strip of tin foil. By reversing the process, the inscriptions on the tin foil reproduced the original sound.

That seems now like a very simple and beautiful idea, but, as in all great inventions, it was profound in its simplicity: it was the first time that words were reproduced directly, without recourse to an alphabet or other symbolic representation. The original model still works. Just as the camera is designed to capture the light waves that are only fleetingly registered on the retina and make them recoverable on a photographic emulsion, so the phonograph was the equivalent direct, self-recording process for the verbal action of the mind.

Eventually, telephone messages ordinarily transmitted by electrical currents along wires were transmitted by radio waves, most recently with the assistance of communication satellites. In view of all these advances in communicating and recording, it is perhaps natural that we should become as much engrossed by the means at our disposal as by the substance of what these means communicate. We are at once overawed and enchanted by the devices themselves, until we come to feel that, compared with modern television, audiovisual tapes, laser scanners that can "read" labels on canned goods, and digital recorders that can convert music into numbers and back again (to say nothing of Christmas cards that can play "Silent Night"), the book, the good old book treasured by our parents and grandparents, looks like something out of date, despite the efforts of type designers to make it look "modern" and worthy of our attention.

Will this taint of being old-fashioned preclude a future for the book? And to ask an even more far-reaching question, Will the new gadgetry destroy the value of literacy? Already, a number of "innovative educators" have publicly asserted that it is no longer important for students to learn to read and write. Meanwhile, in the great audiovisual society that now thrives and spreads to the whole world, some believe that there will be less and less occasion to convey information by writing letters or knowledge by printing books. Hence there will be no need to become proficient in the art of writing. Judging by most of the letters I receive from businesspeople, I would suspect that something new is well on its way as a substitute for thought. Perhaps the word processors of tomorrow will have keys for full paragraphs of clichés, just as electric organs supply ready-made chords for a melody.

At a time when literacy is a "sometime thing" even among college graduates, whole sections of the school curriculum may soon be devoted to what is called "computer literacy." But is it really literacy, and is a computer so difficult to manipulate that it calls for courses with credit? Is it not possible that any present difficulties will be eliminated in the future, thus giving back a little room to basic education? I raise these questions because it is distressing to think that our country may be indulging in the same kind of gadget hysteria that a few years ago filled the classrooms with advanced audiovisual devices, projectors, and so-called teaching machines that are now gathering dust in basements.

The success of the Scribner reference books program on all levels of education persuades us that our basic humanistic assumptions, far from being obsolete, have permanent merit. It is this humanistic outlook that has led to our using the full-length essay form—not the capsule sketch—for the contents of most of our reference sets. We believe that there are important pedagogical advantages in an article that has a beginning, a middle, and an end and that attempts to present the material in its greatest simplicity.

Articles written in the tradition of the humanist—that is, as literature to be read and enjoyed—supply something very different from the flat, toneless inventory of facts that is touted as easy for retrieval from compact discs hooked to a computer. But it was not our objective to give aggregates of facts, bare data. Rather, we were and are seeking to establish for beginners, young and old, ports of entry into various fields of study. We are concerned with *imparting knowledge*, not simply with *storing information* in a package. The former we want to store in human minds.

We at Scribners are not interested in modern methods for "giving access" to the facts in our works by means of retrieval systems. Although we are prepared to cooperate with these mammoth mechanized indexes—they may, in fact, serve research—we have good reason to believe that for learning purposes there is no substitute for one human mind meeting another on the page of a well-written book. For this reason, when people speculate that the libraries of the future will consist exclusively of video monitors linked to computers, I am far from convinced. To the contrary, I believe that the libraries of the future will probably place even more emphasis on books than they do now. Given the intrinsic superiority of literacy to any audiovisual substitute, the book will always retain its unique advantages as a means of instruction. And I include among the advantages its physical form, superior to any screen and set of keys.

It is not sensible, not wise, to think of books as being just another medium of communication, just as it is not sensible to suppose that a telephone call is as satisfactory for all purposes as a letter, that libraries should become "information centers" full of machinery, and that using an audiovisual program will educate as effectively as reading a book. On the lowest level of comparison, a book is in fact a more perfect machine: you do not have to plug it in or give it instructions; it does not glare small batches of green letters into your eyes; you can pick it up and take it anywhere. If you have it in hand, it does not vanish like the text on your screen when the computer system goes "down." For book lovers there is a special kind of excitement in books as physical objects. I remember the great anticipation I felt at the beginning of a new school term—picking up a batch of books, breathing in their newness, and speculating as to their contents—menacing or intriguing—as I set out ready to be filled with new experiences. Some people have been overpowered by this excitement. On seeing for the first time a Shakespeare folio, Charles Lamb was so thrilled that he kissed the book. When I first saw volume 1 of the *Dictionary of Scientific Biography*, I know exactly how he felt. Kissing that book couldn't begin to give adequate expression to my feelings.

Let me argue now for the survival capability of the book from three points of view: the reader, the writer, and society. From the reader's point of view, the value of a great book lies in the demands it makes on him, in addition to whatever he can learn and absorb with ease. Reading is a means of thinking with another person's mind; it forces you to stretch your own. When you are reading a book by a great mind you have to stand on tiptoe, so to speak, to grasp the whole of what is being said. You must adjust the language of your own thoughts to those of the writer. If you succeed, you find your grasp of the language and the quality of your thought permanently enhanced.

In describing a scene a writer may use familiar words, but the visual parts of the description have to be furnished out of your own experience and recomposed in your mind. In turn, when this passage has become part of your experience, it affects the evocative power of the same words when you read another book, while the memory of that book-born vision merges with your later experiences of places and persons, ideas and emotions.

The enormous power of literature lies in that psychological fact. One can infer that, even before the invention of writing, the ancient oral traditions of religious and epic poetry sought to extend the listeners' experiences in this way. By what stronger means could a religious belief be conveyed, or a mythological event be brought to life, than through stories? There is magic in it—as we acknowledge when we say that a book holds us "spellbound." Our attention is so riveted by the action or with concern for the characters that we read on and on, not challenging the most questionable implausibilities. We remain enthralled for hours at a time. No one has ever elucidated that phenomenon more convincingly than Marcel Proust:

> What was my primary, my innermost impulse, the lever whose incessant movements controlled everything else, was my belief in the philosophic richness and beauty of the book I was reading, and my desire to appropriate them for myself, whatever the book might be. . . . For these afternoons were crammed with more dramatic events than occur, often, in a whole lifetime. These were the events taking place in the book I was reading. . . . It matters not that the actions, the feelings appear to us in the guise of truth, since we have made them our own, since it is in ourselves that they are happening, that they are holding in thrall, as we feverishly turn over the pages of the book, our quickened breath and staring eyes. And once the novelist has brought us to this state, for the space of an hour, he sets free within us all the joys and sorrows in the world.

When the English critic Thomas De Quincey spoke of "the literature of power," this effect is what he had in mind. Without trying to, one will remember the place where one was when reading a book, the time of day, the surroundings. Reading can be both a species of shock to the system and a soothing balm. I have recently been reading a number of nineteenth-century novels. Despite the occasional difficulty of getting my mind around some of the complex sentences, it has been like a breath of fresh air to enter a literary world in which the characters have a moral backbone. The cast in the novels of Jane Austen and Trollope and Dickens touch your heart because they portray believable characters caught up in the struggle between their stronger and their weaker natures and emerging with varying fortunes.

As for the impact of books on society, it scarcely needs to be argued. When Abraham Lincoln met Harriet Beecher Stowe he addressed her as the "little lady whose book started this big war." This was an exaggeration, but Lincoln knew that *Uncle Tom's Cabin* had crystallized feelings of abhorrence against slavery in thousands of its readers. In our own time one may cite Steinbeck's *The Grapes of Wrath*, Paton's *Cry, the Beloved Country*, and the novels of Aleksandr Solzhenitsyn as examples of books that have shaped public opinion by powerful representations of good and evil in contemporary life. No one can read Solzhenitsyn's novella *One Day in the Life of Ivan Denisovich* without transforming into live emotions the abstract words "slave-labor camp" and registering lasting visions of its horrors. In a totalitarian regime such a work is inevitably feared and censored. As Solzhenitsyn himself pointed out, a writer may well present the threat of being a second government.

The Bible comprises a collection of books that still retain their extraordinary evocative power and moral impact. Imagine how different the world would have been if the Christian Gospels, instead of presenting the life of Jesus in narrative form, including his own vivid parables, had only been an anthology of his precepts. However complete, could it ever have touched our hearts as deeply?

Stories—the modern novel especially—are also the means of acquainting individuals with the work and the feelings of people outside the range of their occupations. Every class, profession, and age group tends to be isolated and unaware of how the other half lives—and it is much more than a half. It is to the novel that we must go if we want an inside view of a profession such as medicine or acting, of the behavior of the very poor or the enormously rich, of an earlier time or the vision of some distant future period, of some remote part of the world like the Arctic or Tahiti. All these are different worlds accessible in many ways through books and, perhaps most agreeably, through fiction.

For more exact or detailed knowledge, of course, we go to the shelves of treatises in every field from astronomy to zoology. In a book in which the writer acts as a teacher—and this is the case for almost all books categorized as nonfiction—the reader benefits from another's painstaking efforts. The authority has devoted months, years, to a special study, and if he is a competent writer he bears in mind the fact that the reader cannot ask him questions, so he tries to anticipate every question a serious reader might raise and thereby adds to the general understanding of the world.

For the scientist, it is an incalculable benefit to be able to read the original papers of a genius like Einstein, to follow his ideas and his arguments as he blazes a startlingly daring intellectual trail. Someone once asked the great mathematician Abel the secret of his creativity. "Reading the masters" was his reply. By coming close to the thought of a great mind as he consigned it to a book, the searcher of the next generation increases his own powers.

From another point of view, the pedagogical role of the author in simplifying and explaining difficult ideas often strengthens his own understanding of the subject. When an active mind does not put things down on paper, it tends to rest satisfied with what it knows, complacent and comfortable with the obvious. But the task of writing a book for another mind's perusal disabuses the author of some of those comfortable opinions, including those about himself. The American philosopher Charles Peirce said that a good teacher is one who knows the logic of his subject and the psychology of his students. The same demands are made on the writer. Having to make a topic clear to the person "on the other side" of his book, he will have

to struggle, first with expository difficulties and then with difficulties in his subject that were not evident when it lay idle and
untested in his mind. Besides, in describing a situation or an
experiment he will have to walk a tightrope—choosing
between what may be most exact and what may be more vivid.
What a far cry the cerebral performances required by book
writing are from the compilation of facts in a data base.

Finally, the generalized effect of reading on the individuals
composing a society is to sustain the faith in cultures as such. It
is unimaginable that the achievements of Western civilization
could have been continuous and cumulative if books had not
been "lying around," treasured by the intellectually ambitious,
inspiring the young, and enlightening the rest. Before one can
"retrieve" a fact, one must have learned a great deal in a con-
secutive, orderly form. And to extend knowledge one must
know its present boundaries. None of this can be done simply
with information, no matter how fully indexed. Books are pre-
requisite to the articulation of thought. Can we imagine
Jefferson's Declaration of Independence or Lincoln's Gettys-
burg Address being composed without the materials and the
inspiration of the great books—in ethics, philosophy, and political thought?

Reading books, I should add—books, old and new—has the
effect of stabilizing the language from generation to generation.
I know this point of view on language is not popular with lin-
guists, who regard the loss of the meaning of words with the
joy of a doctor at a challenging case. But a rich, subtle, and
clear language is one of the greatest treasures a society can
inherit. Once a word loses its distinctive meaning through
widespread misuse, it is a permanent loss. We are about to lose
the word *fortuitous* in this way. No one would dare to say, for
fear of being misunderstood, "It was fortuitous that my mother-

in-law was there when the bomb went off." But neither can the word be used confidently in the new slovenly and misleading sense. Writers whose business it is to use words in the most reliable way help to keep the language intact by their authority. They are the dikes against the washing away of words. But to serve as such their books have to be read, and they themselves must be readers of books.

The Joys
of Learning

Although my formal education was a classical one—
English, Latin, and Greek—I had always had a special
interest in science, both its subject matter and its
growth. A series published by Henry Schuman known as the
Life of Science Library gave me my first taste for learning the
history of science. These books were written in accessible language and were gems of presentation and particularly useful
for the independent reader or tyro. They were written on a
wide range of subjects. In the exposition, the authors were
careful to temper the wind for the shorn lamb. The books
explored the lives of such figures as Ignaz Semmelweis,
Harvey Cushing, Newton, Darwin, Goethe, and Benjaman
Silliman. Looking back now, it seems to me that these books
were responsible for my growing interest in science.

In my five years as a cryptanalyst in the navy, I was surrounded by people with strong mathematical backgrounds and
who were almost all well grounded in science as well.
Embarrassed by my ignorance in these fields, I undertook a

course of independent study in physics with the help of a marvelous book entitled *Physics—the Pioneer Science*, by Lloyd William Taylor. That book changed my life.

The practice of self-study is age-old, and those who go in for it find a nice balance of advantages between being taught in a classroom and teaching oneself with books. I must confess I find it easier to teach myself a subject. When you encounter a difficulty you have to master it yourself willy-nilly if there's no one around to help you over the rough places. The Greeks had a word for the independent student—*autodidact*—meaning precisely self-taught. Without any reflection upon the curriculum at St. Paul's or Princeton, teaching myself was the greater part of my education. The solutions that one hits upon oneself seem eventually more natural and to the point than those offered by textbook or teacher.

Another pivotal book in my career was *Science and Common Sense* by James B. Conant. A major scientist and president of Harvard University, Conant was especially interested in methods of teaching science to readers with little or no scientific background. One of his sensible ideas for teaching science to beginners was to show them the principles involved in early discoveries of major importance; they are fundamental and at the same time readily understandable. Conant outlined a few sample cases—Robert Boyle's work in pneumatics, Luigi Galvani's and Alessandro Volta's discoveries in electricity, and Antoine Lavoisier's chemical revolution. Later science, and especially that of the twentieth century, requires a more complicated background.

In addition to approaching science in this way, Conant supplied a bibliography that I found enormously helpful, which enabled me to benefit from a course in physics for the autodidact. The list included *Sun, Stand Thou Still: The Life and Work of Copernicus the Astronomer*, by Angus Armitrage; *The*

Nature of Natural History, by Marston Bates; *The Art of Scientific Investigation*, by W. I. B. Beveridge; *The Logic of Modern Physics*, by P. W. Bridgman; *The Origins of Modern Science*, by Herbert Butterfield; *Science, Servant of Man*, by Bernard I. Cohen; *Louis Pasteur, Free Lance of Science*, by René J. Dubos; *Einstein: His Life and Times*, by Philipp Frank; *The Philosophy of William James, Drawn from His Own Works*, by W. Rupert Maclaurin; *Scientists and Amateurs: A History of the Royal Society*, by Dorothy Stimson; *Science and the Modern World*, by A. N. Whitehead; *From Euclid to Eddington*, by Sir Edmund Whittaker; and *The Growth of Scientific Ideas*, by W. P. D. Wightman. In addition, I subscribed to *Isis*, which reviews the new books in the field, and I gradually worked my way through the Life of Science Library, which numbered notable biographies of Copernicus, Ramon y Cajal, and other towering figures.

One of the fruits of this reading was to realize the great variety of ways in which new ideas are arrived at. Some discoveries are made by sharp-eyed observation, others by imaginative applications of logic, and still others at least partly by chance. From reading *The Dreaming Brain*, by J. Allan Hobson, I found how fragments of knowledge are multiplied rather than added together. The bit of neurology that I acquired in reading about Cajal helped me to get more out of *The Dreaming Brain*, and also to appreciate much more fully what Cajal had done.

The pioneer of neuroanatomy Cajal was born in 1852 in the little Spanish village of Petilla, which, in its remoteness and poverty, might now be compared to the most neglected spot in America's Appalachia. Cajal was something of a problem child, with no obvious interests except for an extraordinary gift for drawing. Although his father viewed this talent without enthusiasm, when Cajal finally came to follow in his father's footsteps as a medical student his virtuosity in anatomical drawing gave him the kind of confidence and distinction that often encourages a youth to rise above his contemporaries. Cajal fought in Cuba in the Spanish-American War, and it is disturbing to think that he might have been shot dead by one of Teddy Roosevelt's Rough Riders.

After the war, resuming his career as a physician, he gradually found that his deepest interest lay in research, focusing more and more on the mind and its mechanisms. At great financial sacrifice, he managed to purchase a microscope and continued to study the microscopic parts of the brain. Here again his artistic talents came to his aid, for although he sometimes used microphotography, he preferred recording his findings with detailed pencil drawings.

In Cajal's day, the conventional model for the nervous system was that of a single network by which the various parts of the brain were linked together. It was Cajal's great achievement to demonstrate that the brain resembles rather a cluster of colonies—separate elements to which he gave the name "neurons." He is now recognized as the father of neurology. He studied these individual neurons intently and was able to describe their system of operation. To the amusement of his colleague Charles Scott Sherrington, Cajal at times took a fanciful anthropomorphic view and regarded each of the neurons as tiny personalities, the sum of which he spoke of as a beehive, humming away, acting and interacting in response to stimuli from the outside world as well as from within the mind itself. When other scientists challenged his findings, he took his slides to a scientific meeting and arranged them so that each person present could see with his own eyes Cajal's individual neurons and the laws of their behavior. This sufficed to destroy the network model of his contemporaries.

His ideas had been tested in the field of battle and had prevailed. Cajal shared with Camillo Golgi the 1906 Nobel Prize in physiology and medicine. The reasons Cajal succeeded where others failed were his stubbornness—essential for a pioneer—and his dexterity in producing the various colored stains that made these microscopic objects visible.

George Santayana coined the phrase "the chastity of the intellect" to refer to the scientist's virtue of submission or testing by battle: new ideas are invariably questioned by other scientists, who try to duplicate results by experiment and analysis and thereby confirm or disconfirm the new explanation.

Another example of the value of battle testing occurred in the 1920s and 1930s apropos of psychoanalysis. Freud himself was a brilliant writer and an imaginative thinker, and his ideas about how the mind reacts to the stimulus of frightening or disconcerting experiences caught on with a popularity comparable to the earlier vogues of phrenology and mesmerism. Despite their initial acceptance, Freud's ideas have not been established beyond question by battle testing over the years. More recently, the pseudoscience of extrasensory perception and the belief in other paranormal phenomena became subjects of study at an institute headed by J. B. Rhine at Duke University. In the mid sixties, the great physicist John Wheeler was at the head of the American Association for the Advancement of Science (AAAS), and to him the leading figures in parapsychology applied for recognition as a scientific discipline. They were turned down on the grounds that they had not established their claim that their subject was a science. As Professor Wheeler told me, the AAAS would have readily admitted them as members had they been able to show results that could be duplicated.

It is intriguing to look at the origin of some now widely held views in science. The value of sharp-eyed observation is manifest in the work of John Snow. His great contribution to medicine was the insight that cholera is spread by the contamination of water by fecal matter. His discovery was made entirely by simply observing the circumstances of the cases, without benefit of any established germ theory or use of the microscope. When asked by the authorities in London how cholera could be avoided, his answer was the apparently paradoxical one that the handle should be taken off the town pump, thus preventing the drinking of water that had been contaminated. This discovery, which came early in the history of medicine, can be compared to Edward Jenner's discovery of the value of vaccination with cowpox as a prophylaxis against smallpox. Both Jenner and Snow arrived at their ideas on the basis of common sense and close observation. The results were great and valuable, even though a more exact understanding of these diseases lay far in the future.

To repeat the words of Pasteur, "Chance favors the prepared mind." The history of science is filled with instances of scientists succeeding by significant observation, but they were "lucky" only because their minds were prepared to capitalize on the chance perception. For example, Henry Cavendish discovered the composition of water as an incident in a series of experiments on gases. He had filled a glass retort with common air and with what at the time was referred to as dephlogisticated air, or what we now call hydrogen gas. By putting a stick of burning wood into the retort he not only produced a minor explosion, as was to be expected, but also left little beads of water on the inside walls of the retort, which was *not* expected. Cavendish's sharp eyes did not miss those little beads, and he was thus the first to understand the makeup of water, which every schoolchild knows as H_2O.

Great scientists are almost always compulsive in their absorption, their obsession with problems at the root of their research. In the words of the greatest of all scientists, Isaac Newton, "They are never at rest." Take a simple case. George

Airy was sailing on the Thames when his eyes lit on the little pennant moving back and forth on the bow, partly as a result of the forward motion of the boat. He had been struggling with the problem of stellar aberration, and suddenly he saw in the behavior of the pennant a solution by analogy: the motion of the earth through the heavens was akin to the wind causing the flutter of the pennant.

Not all scientists have the good fortune of being able to make use of such casual observations. I remember hearing a talk by a scientist at the American Philosophical Society who had been engaged in an extraordinary effort to identify the great number of strains of pneumococcus. In the course of his investigation, he noticed quite by chance that one batch of pneumococci seemed to be increasing the quantity of another. Almost immediately he realized that he was dealing with underlying genetic material. At that moment he was on the threshold of discovering DNA, but he didn't follow up on his insight and thus missed one of the shiniest of all the brass rings in science.

Yet another case takes us back to Thomas Alva Edison, world famous for his development of the light bulb. Noticing that many of his bulbs were turning black after a while, he had the bright idea of putting a charged metal plate inside the bulb with the thought that this would concentrate the blackening in one place. On examining the results, he came upon the unexpected fact that a current was passing across the open space inside the heated bulb. This phenomenon is now called thermionic emission. But Edison was an excessively practical man and his attention was confined to improving the light bulb. While he made a notation in his notebook about his discovery—now called the Edison effect—its value in use was brought out entirely by the work of other scientists, in particular Lee De Forest.

A final example of a scientist who made a life-saving discovery without benefit of theoretical foundation is the Hungarian physician Ignaz Semmelweis. He came to see that the horrifying prevalence of childbed fever in his hospital was the result of the doctors infecting their patients by means of contaminated material—predominantly from autopsies—on their own hands. He noticed that a young colleague got an infected cut and died of a raging fever in almost exactly the same way that the women were dying in the hospitals. By being sharp-eyed— he associated that the young man died with the same symptoms and course of illness—he made the leap that all these women were dying from the same cause. Conventional wisdom had blamed childbed fever on unhealthy miasmas, and in making his point Semmelweis antagonized the Viennese physicians so bitterly by implicating their sanitary habits that he was pretty well drummed out of organized medicine. He now stands as a medical martyr. Interestingly, Oliver W. Holmes, Sr., made the same discovery as Semmelweis.

I have become chiefly interested in physics and have made a more than desultory study of Einstein's great achievements. The more one learns about his work and his scientific imagination, the more towering his achievements appear, as I discovered when preparing my paper on Henri Poincaré and the theory of relativity for the *American Journal of Physics* in 1964. When I was three or four years old, someone in the household asked me a question that I found difficult to answer. My reply was, "Who do you think I am, Einstein?" The reason for this clincher was that at that time Einstein was reaping his greatest publicity throughout the world. It was natural that my family should be talking about him, unconcerned that little pitchers have big ears.

Einstein in the 1920s was given a ticker-tape parade in virtually every major city of the United States, which for the shy person he was must have been a daily torment. I had seen film clips of his landing in New York and getting off the boat surrounded by photographers with their flashbulbs. He referred to them as *licht affen* or "light monkeys"—all things considered, an excellent word for their profession. Einstein's goodwill tour was to build publicity and financial support for the establishment of a Jewish homeland in Israel. The tour coincided with the enormous prestige of his unparalleled scientific achievements, about which the average person knew as much as I did when I retorted, "Who do you think I am. . . ." Einstein's success not only made him a world figure, but also conferred the glamour on a scientific achievement comparable to Newton's theory of gravitation two centuries earlier.

Einstein was living in Princeton, at the Institute for Advanced Studies, when I was an undergraduate at the university. One day, my professor of German told me that he could arrange a lunch with me and either Thomas Mann or Professor Einstein. I was studying Thomas Mann at the time and was inclined to meeting him. In a decision that is still agonizing to me, I opted for Herr Mann, who turned out to be pretentious and deadly boring, whereas everything I have heard about Einstein indicates that he would have been full of life and fun. Any Nobel Prize winner who is, moreover, one of the great scientists of all time and walks up the main street of Princeton eating an ice cream cone must have an engaging, unpretentious personality.

One day, still in Princeton, I was coming back from rowing on Lake Carnegie and happened upon Professor Einstein and his sister Maja walking together, each flaunting an impressive halo of white hair. The great man had stopped on the road and was looking at some object with sustained attention. He prodded it briefly with his walking stick before moving on. I was curious to see what had arrested his attention and strolled on to where he had stopped. I found only a flattened dried-out toad that had obviously been run over by an automobile. It was not, I thought, a very interesting object of study, but who can comprehend the curiosity of an Einstein?

During the war, a friend of his from Germany called Beckey entertained him in Watch Hill, Rhode Island, where Einstein would walk up the beach, pausing to reflect on the different density of packing of the sand in and out of the water. His host's car—indeed, all American cars—was to him a scandalous waste of energy. He thought there was no need of such tremendous horsepower for ordinary transportation, and he viewed these objects of our pride with something like contempt. At that time I don't suppose there was more than a handful of Americans who viewed cars as wasteful machines, but now Einstein's opinion has been gaining ground. In the lovely phrase of Loren Eiseley, he was a man who saw through time.

When did Einstein's interest in science begin? He himself suggested that it may have been when he was a little boy of four or five and his father gave him a compass. He took it in his hands and was filled with wonder that no matter which way he turned the compass, the needle kept pointing in the same direction. Obviously some mysterious and invisible force was acting on the needle to hold it in place. For the rest of his life, Einstein never lost that sense of the mystery of nature which he had felt as a child playing with that compass. As an older boy he would think up imaginary experiences and puzzle over them. What would happen if you traveled so fast that you caught up with a ray of light? What would be different then?

Another formative experience in Einstein's boyhood was his discovery of the power of mathematics. He was about nine or ten years old when a young medical student who was a friend of the family brought him a geometry text filled with facts and problems about triangles, circles, and straight lines. The boy found it a beautiful science. You could prove by simple argument that something had to be true, and all the truths hung together. Young Albert was eager to test himself and see whether he could prove some of these remarkable truths without help. As he grew older his love of mathematics endured and helped him enormously in arriving at his scientific conclusions.

By the time he was sixteen his interest in science was so strong that he was planning a series of experiments to discover the nature of the ether, a mysterious substance that was supposed to fill the universe. Since light consisted of waves, it had to have something to travel in, much as sound waves travel in air or ripples in the water of a pond. But it was the Americans, Michelson and Morley, not Einstein, who finally disposed of the ether in 1887.

When Einstein was a young graduate student he not only read widely in his chosen field of physics, but he also pursued an active interest in the writings of such great modern philosophers as Kant and Hume. On his own testimony, this enabled him to deal with some of the puzzles and paradoxes of science, but he also makes it clear that philosophy owes a reciprocal debt to physics, particularly with respect to the concept of time. To paraphrase him, the physicist had to bring the concept of time down to earth from the Parnassus of the philosophical a priori in order to put it in working condition for science.

I remember hearing that once, in the 1930s, the son of one of Einstein's friends was deeply depressed as a result of the philosophical conviction that life had no meaning. The father in desperation introduced him to Einstein, with the hope that that wise old man might say something to cure the son's world-weariness. Einstein looked at the boy with surprise and said,

"How could you not wish to go on living when we still don't know all there is to know about light?" I have no idea what impact this point of view had on the boy, but it illustrates how the study of light was a source of enduring challenge and joy to Einstein. He had the supreme joy of making a wholly original contribution to our understanding of the nature of light in what was later known as his photon theory. Newton himself had tentatively accepted a particle theory of the propagation of light, although in later time it was superseded by a wave theory. But not all the manifestations of light could be explained in that way. To meet this difficulty Einstein hit upon the revolutionary idea that light should also be thought of as a stream of tiny particles of energy. For each particle the amount of energy depends on the frequency—that is, on the color—of the light. It was a daring suggestion, but he was able to support his view with the corroboration of other light phenomena. The most impressive of these is the so-called photoelectric effect, by which a quantum of light bombarding a piece of metal displaces an electron and produces a tiny electric current. Today our light meters in photography, our television tubes, and many of our copying machines are based on this property of light.

One sees the photoelectric effect in action when at an airport the door opens automatically. For this discovery Einstein was awarded the Nobel Prize in 1921. Decades later, in 1979, the German government issued a postage stamp commemorating this achievement with a little diagram explaining how it works. I have it framed on my desk.

Another problem Einstein tackled had to do with the laws of electricity. It seemed impossible to fit those laws into a single theory that would also include the laws of mechanics. Mechanics is the science of material bodies in motion, from the orbits of the planets around the sun to the motions of the tiny molecules in a liquid or a gas. The laws of mechanics all state that the motion of a body is always *relative* motion. Thus a car may be traveling sixty miles an hour relative to the highway but over sixty thousand miles an hour relative to the sun. You cannot tell how fast a body is "really" traveling in space; you can only describe how fast one body is traveling in relation to another. That is why if you are on a smoothly moving boat or train you can think of yourself as being "at rest," and experiments in mechanics on the boat or train will come out the same as if they were performed in a laboratory on the ground. This is the *principle of relativity*.

In his reminiscences Albert Einstein describes the agony he suffered in his search for what was later known as his theory of relativity. He would sometimes go off on long trips in the countryside of Switzerland to alleviate the strain of his mental efforts. This turned out to be a wonderful decision, because once, on the way home, he ran into two of his friends who asked him how his theory was faring. "I have given it up," he said. "It seems hopeless." When asked what the trouble was, he began to explain his difficulty, and in the process he saw the idea that had eluded him. The whole solution unfolded itself to him. "It was like a thunderstorm," he said.

Unlike most scientists, Einstein assumed that electrical and magnetic effects, as well as the behavior of light, depended only on relative motions. He was able to show how all these laws, as well as the laws of mechanics, could be brought together into a single theory. That was the great step forward. He also showed that the idea of the ether, which he had pondered as a boy, could now be dropped altogether.

Perhaps the most important result of Einstein's theory of relativity was to reveal that matter and energy are two different forms of the same thing. A tiny amount of matter is the equivalent of a huge amount of energy. That is the meaning of the famous equation $E = mc^2$. Einstein was able to use this knowledge to explain the energy released continuously by radioactive substances like uranium and radium. Later the equivalence of matter and energy made possible the development of nuclear power. It was an idea that changed the world.

If I were asked for a single characteristic that made Einstein so great a genius, I would name his boldness. His thought processes were always daring. Over and over again he took a point of view of unprecedented originality. This trait is connected with a firm reliance on the principle known as Occam's razor. Let me explain. In the course of my reading I came across a letter from the great American physicist Josiah Willard Gibbs to a friend of his who was congratulating him on the progress he had made in his scientific research. Gibbs replied that he was very much pleased by this praise, because in the theoretical field in which he worked it was not always easy to recognize an authentic advance of the kind that does not lead to an obvious step forward but yields only the advantage of a new way of attacking problems. As Gibbs went on to say, one of the principal objects of theoretical research is to find the point of view from which the subject appears in its greatest simplicity.

This search for the greatest simplicity in ideas dates back at least to the Middle Ages, when the philosopher and scientist William of Occam laid down the principle: "*Essentiae praeter necessitatem non multiplicandae sunt.*" We would translate this as "You should not introduce more assumptions than are absolutely necessary," or keep ideas as simple as possible. That slogan has been nicknamed Occam's razor—it cuts away the superfluous. I think this principle ought to be inscribed upon the frieze of every institution of higher learning.

Einstein was a lifelong user of Occam's razor. Time and again he would criticize or at least be unhappy with a hypothesis that seemed to him ugly and wrong because it was so complicated.

And time and again he boldly made scientific progress by thinking up a simpler and more beautiful solution. In his inimitable way, he remarks on what to him was the puzzling fact that we wonder about things that we observe. That gift of wonderment may be one further manifestation of our powers of speech, which we exercise continually in our mental life—that is, in the unending conversations we have with ourselves. Wondering can be a joy of sorts. It certainly draws our attention to the richness of the world we live in. Assessing Einstein's genius, it seems to me that there are two sides to it—one imaginative and speculative and the other possessing acute, critical powers. Interestingly, some years ago my sister Julia presented me with a superb drypoint etching of Einstein. This portrait shows these two different aspects his face could assume: one depicting a glazy expression signifying the contemplative and speculative side and the other sharp-eyed, demonstrating a critical acuity.

In my role as publisher, I have felt grateful for the knowledge and pleasure I have derived from working with some of our scientific writers. One of our famous interpreters of physics, James Trefil, told me about the book *The Cartoon Guide to Genetics*, by Larry Gonick and Mark Wheelis. He found it fascinating, and I must say that he did not exaggerate the intellectual joy of acquiring a deeper understanding of the whole field of genetics in a painless and satisfying way. Another book Dr. Trefil told me of is one on light by Hazel Rossotti entitled *Colour*, published by Princeton University Press; it is excellent and can be easily comprehended by almost any reader.

Publishing the *Dictionary of Scientific Biography* was truly the fulfillment of my passionate interest in the history of science, which Conant's book first ignited. With my mind full of somewhat confused ideas as to a desirable publication, I wrote to Dr. Charles Gillispie of Princeton University asking to see him. I had not met him but was familiar with his splendid book *The Edge of Objectivity*. I told him that I wanted to discuss a project in his field and had been "nursing the hope" that he would assist us as an advisory editor. He responded courteously, and I visited him at Princeton a few days later. I look upon that visit as eventful as Dr. Watson's first meeting with Sherlock Holmes.

The principal purpose of the *DSB* was to describe the achievements of individual scientists from the earliest times to the present day, but I consider the dictionary as much a humanistic as a scientific work—that is, I hold to the idea that humanism is a point of view that can be taken toward all departments of knowledge, including science. From the humanistic point of view, the creation of increasingly comprehensive and beautiful schemes in science, the production of more and more precise scientific data, and the continual application of scientific knowledge to practical human needs are all coordinated achievements in the life of the mind and additions to the contents of human experience.

I would say further that no matter how complex or unfamiliar the subject matter of a particular science may become, or how far its concepts and assumptions may be at variance with our ordinary intuition, the thought processes of scientists are not fundamentally different from those of other researchers in other departments of knowledge, who must apply imagination, reason, and factual investigation to whatever difficulties of understanding arise in their work. In this connection one thinks of the simple definition of scientific method proposed by the physicist Percy Bridgman. He called it "Doing your damndest with your mind—no holds barred."

My concern and my reading in science did not disappear after the publication of the *DSB*; my curiosity has never waned.

Even today I cannot stop myself from daydreaming about the books that are still to be published and the possible reference books that have not yet seen the light of day.

My interest in the history of science has been an intellectual adventure that has led me on delightful visits to England. On one occasion, my wife and I made a pilgrimage to Isaac Newton's home in the company of a young Marshall scholar studying the history of science, Jennifer Tucker. My first impressions of Newton's home was how much the landscape, dirt roads, and hedgerows reminded me of scenes in the American Berkshires. To see Newton's homeplace was a realization of an almost lifelong dream to pay homage to the great man. Unfortunately, in my enthusiasm I rushed headlong into his house, almost braining myself on the lintel of the door. It seemed so unfair that Newton was threatened only by having an apple fall on his head, while I was threatened by being decapitated by the lintel. The Royal Society not only allowed me to look through Newton's initial little reflecting telescope but also to satisfy myself that it was still in working condition. How much that would have delighted the inventor, although knowing Newton, he would have been quick to see opportunities for further improvement.

It was a thrill to visit the Cambridge University Library where the Scribner reference books were all well represented and apparently frequently used by students from every department of knowledge. I was invited to lead an open seminar in publishing for graduate students at Gonville and Caius College at Cambridge. There I dined with such noted scholars in the field of the history of science as Dr. Michael Redhead and Dr. Simon Schaffer, whose book *Leviathan and Air Pump* had been published by Princeton University Press. After several visits I came to identify myself with the Cambridge History of Science

Department as a visiting scholar; for me the greatest treat would have been to sit in on one of Michael Redhead's seminars.

Until the nineteenth century, a scientist was described as a natural philosopher. When Dickens poked fun at an astronomer in *The Pickwick Papers* he naturally used the word "philosopher" in the sense that we today would refer to a scientist. It is only recently that the phrase "natural philosophy" has been renamed science, and I think it is a pity and a shame that the link between abstract thought and scientific inquiry has been discarded. The philosophical roots of our modern scientific tradition repay study and meditation—as Einstein's example proves. With the philosophical background, one is all the better able to walk in the footsteps of the discoverers, to share intimately some of the joys of their intellectual adventure.

III

Then and Now

Proustian
Remembrances

❧

In describing the child's capacity to learn, the late neuro-surgeon Wilder Penfield coined the phrase "the uncommit-ted cortex." By that he was referring to the special capacity for learning shown by children roughly between the ages of two and thirteen—from infancy to adolescence. Perhaps as another faculty of the uncommitted cortex, many memories of childhood, but not infancy, survive in our minds with extraordinary tenacity. It seems that the memory operates on a first-in/last-out inventory system, often to our satisfaction but often to our embarrassment. I can still remember the list of Latin prepositions compounded with the verbs that take the dative or indirect object, but I sometimes have trouble remembering my telephone number.

Our lives are filled with the mysterious workings of the mind. Not a day goes by without some data of the past floating by in the stream of consciousness, coming and going as natural-ly and unbidden as a leaf falling from a tree. This reminds us that the mind has autonomous powers and stores far more of our past than we can ever review.

It was his preoccupation with this phenomenon that inspired Proust's great novel, *Remembrance of Things Past*, partly a work of art and partly a work of scientific investigation. I am afraid that my memories of childhood have neither the scientific nor the artistic vision that inspired Proust, yet these almost Proustian memories continue to frequent and influence my daily thoughts and actions.

When the Great Depression began in 1929 I was eight years old. Inevitably, some of the results of this huge catastrophe impinged on our lives, but as the result of my family's acquired means it created virtually no individual hardship for us. While most of the traumas of the period were seen by us from a distance, as from the wrong side of a telescope, the suffering I witnessed nevertheless left me with poignant, lasting images.

Where the Newark International Airport now stands there was a huge, virtual town of little shacks made from tarpaper and crates. There were so many of them on the landscape that soon this whole area was referred to as "Hooverville," which carried an obvious political sting. It was a drabness without any element of joy.

In Concord, New Hampshire, where I was a boarding student, the shops were pitifully bare of anything but the most shabby goods. It was the bone-shabbiness of the period. A number of my schoolmates had to drop out because they could no longer pay the tuition. I don't suppose this was an ultimate catastrophe, but certainly a humiliation and a setback for a young boy.

I recall the trucks carrying young men that used to rumble through the Berkshires—New Marlborough, Massachusetts— where my family spent the summers. These were the recruits for the Civilian Conservation Corps (CCC) that Roosevelt had established. The object was to create work and therefore give sustenance to young men in their early or late teens (who might otherwise be seriously undernourished). The CCC camps were run by army officers, one of whom was Colonel Elting, who retired and became a professor at West Point and a prolific writer of military history. Responsible for a number of worthwhile projects, the CCC had a group that we saw in Massachusetts which was charged with creating a substantial dam and what is now York Lake. Organizing these camps turned out to be a truly fine idea, and it is quite clear in retrospect that the CCC served an important practical as well as humanitarian role. Besides, the CCC created a lasting bond among its young recruits, many of whom became prominent in American public life. (As a sidelight, I am told an alumni group still exists.) In some respects the CCC is analogous to the Peace Corps, insofar as it tapped the energies and enthusiasm of the young generation.

Several federal programs were set up to give some paying jobs to unemployed persons. Many of these jobs were manual labor such as cleaning the streets and other low-level work. I remember more fortunate people making wisecracks about men on relief and working at these jobs. Some were sneered at because they worked so slowly. One lampoon referred to them as "roadside statues." It pains me now to realize that many of those men worked so lethargically and did so little because they could not afford to eat well enough to keep up a more active pace. In retrospect, I wish I could be pardoned for my blindness to their plight.

The hardships of unemployment for young people during the depression were recognized as catastrophic and were dealt with by drastic and imaginative expedients. In the light of our own time and its problems, it strikes me as sad that nothing similar has been established for the youth of today, who face the substantially greater dangers and lures of drugs and crime. Roosevelt, thou shouldst be living at this hour!

Some of the most poignant evidence of the catastrophic character of the Great Depression could be found in small things. On the sidewalks of Park Avenue stood a number of men, each with a stand and a little pile of apples to sell. It was dismaying to see so many people selling apples. They were obviously terribly poor, but one could see from their clothing that this had not always been the case. The incongruity was appalling—these men in their not-yet-worn-out business suits struggling to survive as peddlers. My mother was punctilious about buying an apple from every stand. The sale took the curse off begging.

One cook, like many others in our area of Far Hills, New Jersey, used to feed the beggars who would go from door to door. One such man, called "the country gentleman," had lost all his money when the market crashed and was now reduced to dressing up in his best clothes and going to the houses of the wealthy. Most of these home owners never knew that this went on. On the whole, though, people were more kindly to the poor in that area because they felt closer to them, viewing them more as neighbors down on their luck than as beggars. Since that time I have come to the conclusion that wealthy people are often more horrified of destitution than people who grew up in impoverished neighborhoods and were acquainted with it. I note it in some politicians who grew up with silver spoons in their mouths but were transformed by their contact with poverty—an encounter that came to define their liberalism.

Personal testimony always moves one more than newspaper reports. One of our company salesmen once told me of his taking all the household silver and hocking it to buy food for his family. People would come into the Children's Book Department at Scribners with the pitiful hope of selling stories that had no prospect of being published. It was disheartening to our children's book editor, willing but unable to help.

For my part, I confess to seeing shadows of the depression without realizing their significance. I still recall my disbelief at seeing a boy I knew steal a piece of fruit from a load being delivered to my family's icehouse in the Berkshires. I was shocked to learn that this boy was facing such poverty that he needed to pilfer fruit for nourishment.

Another image I have never forgotten is that of a hunch-backed old man, with a bag weighing some thirty pounds over one shoulder, walking miles up Lamington Road near our New Jersey house with dignity and courage. This peddler, Willie Wise, would take the train down from Newark into Far Hills and would then walk for several miles or hitchhike from house to house on his regular route. In later years if I saw him hitch-hiking I would give him a ride. Perhaps in the afterlife this might spare me some of the torments of Lazarus, but I didn't do it with that in mind. He dealt mostly in wares and toiletries for the stable hands. The grooms in turn would sometimes try to sell him their watches, claiming they were gold. This claim would occasion a scientific routine. Willie would take the watch and with a tiny whetstone make a scratch on the case. He would then pour a small amount of nitric acid on the mark. If the watch was truly gold, the scratch was unaffected by the acid and the deal was made. No one ever got the better of Willie Wise.

This was also the era of Father Charles Coughlin, a horrify-ingly bigoted rabble-rouser. He had a national radio program, originating from Royal Oak, Michigan, which he used to vilify everyone connected with Wall Street or anyone Jewish as being responsible for the market crash. As a young boy, I would see my family's grooms gathered together in the tack room listening to Father Coughlin on the radio as he blasted

Franklin Roosevelt. This demagogue became so outrageous he was finally silenced by his bishop.

The indignities of the depression were not easy to describe by those who suffered or witnessed them, and, as a result, a division emerged between generations—those who had lived through the evil time and those who had not. Some people who lived through the depression tended to be frugal and cautious, which often made the attitudes of younger generations that hadn't shared the upheaval and its privations seem relatively devil-may-care. My own family's affluence amid the suffering of other Americans left me with a sense of privilege and corresponding feelings of obligation and guilt. This in turn has often caused me to blame myself for mistakes or unkindnesses that were unintended or unanticipated. I first felt these pangs growing up with our household staff.

When I was five or six years old, my family employed an Italian gardener who came to work on the place by the day and to stoke the furnace. Because his name was relatively unpronounceable for me, I gave him the name Joe-Boy, a name that stuck and was adopted by the whole family. Joe-Boy had been a soldier in the Italian infantry in World War I, and he taught me some of the marching songs of the Italian army. One of these songs was acted out by crossing each other's arms and swinging each around at the end of the song. I do not clearly remember all the words of the song, but it started something like *All'armi! La guerra* and ended with a sound something like "pa pa pa boom." I don't think that Joe-Boy liked the "pa pa pa boom" part of war, and I don't blame him, but it was quite a spellbinding performance for me.

Joe-Boy was arranging for his wife to immigrate to the United States, and a number of letters arrived from Italy in connection with her purpose. I was given the stamps from all these letters, and no subsequent work of visual arts has struck me as being quite as beautiful as those Italian stamps.

As a bored preschooler, I found tagging behind Joe-Boy to be a daily joy. The only exception was when I saw him carrying two ducks upside down and seeing him wring their necks simultaneously with a brutal twisting motion. Some people might consider this a traumatic experience, but I doubt that it was. For one thing, it was all over so quickly, almost before I knew what was happening. In any case, I'm not sure it is a bad idea for us to realize that the flesh we eat comes from animals that did not die a natural death. I think it interesting that an almost identical incident is described by Proust, in which the cook Françoise exhibited such a heartless approach to life. I believe it made a big impact on Proust to see this sadistic act of slaughtering the chickens.

I spent hours with Joe-Boy and often ate a bite or two of the sandwich he brought in his lunchbox. It seemed better to me than any of the food I was given at home. One day I asked Joe-Boy for a piece of chewing gum called a Chiclet, but Joe-Boy thought I was asking for a nickel, and he gave it to me, much to the mortification of my family. I was pleased that Joe-Boy had been willing to give me the nickel in the first place. My boyhood was restrained all around by rules of behavior, and obviously, in the eyes of my parents, this transaction constituted a serious faux pas on my part.

It would be impossible to talk about the time in which I grew up without mentioning the character and institutions of my hometown of Far Hills, New Jersey. These small memories constitute to a large degree what the 1930s meant to me.

I was brought up in a building we called "The Old Stone House," otherwise referred to as the Mellick Farm, an inn dating back to the Revolution. In the cellar was a massive fireplace that, in the eighteenth century, served the patrons of the inn. Going to or from New York involved a ferry ride across the Hudson River, whether you traveled by car or train. To get to work in New York, my father would take the Delaware and Lackawanna Railroad to Hoboken, and from there he would take a ferry to downtown Manhattan. The ferry ride was a treat for me, but with the completion of the center portion of the Lincoln Tunnel in 1937 the ferry soon stopped running. The commuter trains were all powered by steam locomotives, and the sight of them in the station always produced a little shiver of excitement. Some of us children would put pennies on the track to watch them be flattened by the wheels. Electric trains can't do that—I know because I've tried.

From time to time historic events were occasions for community celebration. One of the most colorful was the 1933 bicentennial of the birth of George Washington. As a special feature, some of the local horsemen were dressed in the costumes of the Revolution and rode through Peapack and Gladstone to the accompaniment of fifes and drums. Roger Mellick represented George Washington and rode my father's white horse, Moonshine. Other characters in the march were Lafayette and Rochambeau. No one will ever forget that parade.

Old-fashioned general stores, like Lance's in Far Hills, played important community roles during this period; they sold every kind of merchandise from groceries, bolts of cloth, and candy to pots and pans and marbles for that same clientele. Mr. Lance's delivery man, Clarence, used to speed down Lamington Road, then unpaved, in a rickety delivery truck that resembled a matchbox on wheels.

Some of our Far Hills neighbors, including my good friend John Pierrepont, attended a private school that in their memories was frighteningly Dickensian. It was run by the Reverend

James Hollywood Stone Fair and his wife, Rosalie Moran Fair. Mr. Fair called it the Somerset Hills Preparatory School, but the name never stuck. Everyone called it just the Fair School. My sister Julia and I attended it without any permanent educational damage. One interesting thing was the range of ages of the pupils. The oldest, named Bucko Jones, seems in memory to have been in size and age a candidate for the New York Giants, while some of the rest of us were pitifully preadolescent. To be just to Mr. Fair, we were given *some* education—some grounding in Latin and an understanding of English grammar that proved quite satisfactory. The teaching of French was clearly above our heads. I remember one textbook, *L'Armour du Magyar*, a story about the armaments of Hungary of which not a single word or event was even faintly comprehensible. Perhaps that dreadful thing is still being taught to beginners in French. I hope they get more out of it than I did. There was also an introductory Latin course that I think deserves a B+ since there was nothing to unlearn when I went to boarding school. The arithmetic was basically a bundle of algorithms that provided a number of procedures for solving problems but supplied no understanding of how the operation worked. Thus, I would say A is to B as B is to C and follow that up by multiplying means and extreme. We got the right answer, but it was no better than a magician's trick—cookbook education and worth very little.

Our introduction to literature was unsatisfactory because we were asked to read more sophisticated books than most of us could digest. In some cases the reading level was beyond our ability. Floundering in a book one cannot comprehend is bewildering and possibly contributes a quantum of dyslexia; it certainly did not impart any habits of successful or pleasurable reading.

One source of my compulsory reading at that time was an anthology of martial poems entitled *Lyra Heroica*, containing great potboilers like "Horatius at the Bridge" and other immortal works. For many decades I mistranslated that title as though *lyra* were a neuter plural, so that in my mind each poem was a *lyrum*. Another of the heroic poems we read in class was one, I think, by Richard Lovelace entitled "To Lucasta, on Going to the Wars," which contained the deathless lines:

> But this inconstancy is such
> as thou too shalt adore
> I could not love thee, dear, so much
> Loved I not honor more.

I felt like giving a Bronx cheer after the fact. Any normal "dear" would resent taking second place in this way.

Other stories we read included a particularly gloomy one entitled *The Man without a Country*. In it a soldier was condemned by the powers that be to spend the rest of his life on a ship without seeing his country again—all this for saying "Damn the United States" in a fit of anger. Only after his death was it discovered that his cabin was filled with U.S. memorabilia and an American flag lay under his pillow.

In some ways Mr. Fair was very imaginative in developing certain skills in his students. Somewhere in the history of his school he had hired a Colonel Edwards, an ex–cavalry officer whose son also worked for the school. Both of them were experts in riding, and the older boys were taught all kinds of equestrian skills, most suitable for the horsey community of Far Hills. Some of these equestrians were able to sit backwards on a horse when it jumped over a fence, to jump blindfolded, and to perform all kinds of acrobatic feats on top of the horse, no matter how disconcerting to the latter; and, as I recall, no one sustained any injury from these daring displays.

Another source of entertainment was singing in the classroom—I mean, at appropriate times. I remember learning a collection of popular ballads—"There's a Tavern in the Town," "Clementine," and others. My favorite was "A Capital Ship for an Ocean Trip Was the Walloping Windowblind." It had such memorable verses as "No wind that blew disturbed the crew or troubled the captain's mind," which is probably the American answer to "The Volga Boat Song." I can still sing modestly off-key all of these songs taught to us by a Mr. Marsh; they are still a trial to my sons.

One of the figures most loved by the children of the community, and regarded as something of a saint by their parents, was Dr. Kay, a slender man with a rather nasal voice and a permanent odor of disinfectant. His practice was entirely limited to house calls, and he always appeared as promptly as he could in a little black sedan. Dr. Kay was a general practitioner with a capital G—he sewed up wounds, set bones, and delivered babies.

The talented and devoted student of science and literature Dr. Lewis Thomas has provided a persuasive account of the limitations of medicine before the advent of scientific research in the field in the forties. As he points out, great reliance had to be placed on the medicinal powers of nature itself. Beyond that, the doctors had to settle for placebos in the form of brightly colored pills. Dr. Kay was aware of this truth, and his medicine bag was fitted, as I remember, with three tiers of shelving that expanded like an accordion to reveal these eye-catching placebos. I still remember his repeated warnings that the patient should "force the fluids," which meant drinking great quantities of water or ginger ale. In less serious situations he could probably depend on a placebo to satisfy the need for action. In very serious cases, he would be obliged to take the course of watchful waiting. The handicap he was under was enormous compared with the resources of modern-day medicine. So many diseases that once were life-threatening are now treatable thanks to the rather miraculous effects of the antibiotics that appeared in the forties.

The first time my family called Dr. Kay to treat me in my childhood was after I had complained one afternoon of an earache that seemed to become more and more painful. In some fearfulness, the family asked Dr. Kay to come over. Visiting me in my bedroom, Dr. Kay examined my eardrum and saw a situation, referred to in the colorful language of the time as a "gathered ear." This meant an infection behind the eardrum causing a certain amount of pus and a great deal of pain. One of the most frightening of all diseases in those days was an infection of the mastoid bone; it was frequently fatal, I suppose because of its proximity to the brain. Dr. Kay's decision was to puncture the eardrum as a means of draining away the discharge, thereby reducing the pressure. Since he could not perform this easily on a child without anesthesia, he chose to put me to sleep with ether, right in my bed. First, he poured ether over something that looked like a sieve lined with gauze, which he held over my nose and mouth. This anesthetized me almost at once. For a few seconds I was gagging and struggling to breathe, at which point I remember his saying as gently as he could, "I'll give you a breath of air" and he removed the ether for an instant, but by then I was out. I can still remember the strange sounds created by my brain as I regained conciousness. Curiously, this frightening experience never induced in me any fear of Dr. Kay.

Of course no discussion of the ways of the community in the 1930s would be complete without some mention of the early movie houses, of which there were a great many in the region. In Morristown alone there may have been as many as six or seven, all relatively small and strategically situated next to drugstores with soda fountains, which contributed yet another part to the pleasure of moviegoing. I remember the Liberty in

Bernardsville, the smallest of them all, yet the only one still running. Eventually a movie house called the Community Theatre was built in Morristown; it was bigger and more ornate than anything around—it resembled an Arabian Night's dream. My friends and I thought of the place as a miracle of architecture; we felt spiritually elevated at the sight of it.

But all these country theaters paled in comparison with the stupendous palaces of New York City—the Roxy, Loew's Lexington, Radio City Music Hall, to mention a few. An outstanding merit of the New York theaters was their elaborate musical effects. Before the feature film, the lights would dim and a full symphony orchestra would resound, to visual effects using the whole spectrum of colors, red gradually changing to blue by some elaborate mechanism. It was a magnificent show even before the movie began, and it lifted us to a cultural plateau of mingled sense perceptions that we could not have reached otherwise.

By far the most awe inspiring was Radio City Music Hall, the absolute epitome of movie theater glamour. I felt so important and grown up as I climbed the huge staircase from the ground level and sat back in one of the plush chairs. Like everyone else I was mesmerized by the Rockettes, who achieved a level of mechanical precision that seemed almost supernatural.

One of the most popular movies of the day was a 1925 Lon Chaney horror film, *The Phantom of the Opera.* My parents were far too enlightened to allow me to see it, knowing I would never recover from the fright. But I was so obsessed by the title alone that I spent weeks making up plots involving phantoms and operas without seeing a single frame of the movie.

As we got older our parents were not as concerned about shielding us from scary movies, and my friends and I witnessed some terrifying examples of the genre. The one that frightened me the most was *Dr. X* (1932). One of Dr. X's modes of disguise was to put on his face synthetic flesh of the most gruesome kind. Somehow Dr. X had inveigled a group of people into letting him lock them tight in a row of electric chairs, and only the presence of mind of a rather comical reporter rescued them. The heroine was Fay Wray, who acted in every film that called for a screaming woman. She was Hollywood's most talented screamer and starred in *King Kong* (1933). The ape was very taken with her despite their egregious difference in size and species.

All these adventures at the movies and in movie houses provided a background to which many later experiences have attached themselves. We had grown up under the spell of the movies—note that this is what they were, not "films"—and our very imaginations were shaped and colored by the big screen and even bigger "palaces."

Perhaps one of my most formative experiences occurred when my parents were in Europe and I was staying with my grandparents. I bought a copy of *Popular Mechanics* for twenty-five cents. This magazine sparked a beginning interest in virtually all fields of science, technology, and the "manual arts." On that issue's cover was a picture of a dirigible; the inside was filled with articles about all kinds of new things being made and about projects you could undertake at home. The fantasies it induced about making things, coupled with my new, inextinguishable interest in science, led my family, who had planned on my going into publishing, to fear that I might become an engineer or—worst of all—a mechanic.

A few years ago, when up in Maine and talking with Ambassador Henry Villard, a fellow combatant of Ernest Hemingway's in the First World War, I mentioned *Popular Mechanics*, never imagining that he read it. He surprised me by saying he too found it an endlessly interesting source of information about what was going on in science and technology. I said, "I think there's the basis for a secret fraternity here." I am a believer in the virtue of crafts. It is good for the morale and for the enjoyment of the world around you to have made some objects with your own hands.

After studying Isaac Newton's career, I am convinced that his early success in building and drawing was an important factor in his development as a great scientist. Adolescents who cultivate manual skills have something particularly precious in an age when everything is simply bought in stores. Learned skills that have an artistic component are good for the soul, and indeed are important for the country, which should not be totally preoccupied with the business side of life, important as that is. Alongside the gross national product we should have something called the gross national artistic output. It would let loose the first salvo against the Philistines and might well raise the nationwide level of creativity and happiness.

The first time I picked up a radio signal on my crystal set I thought I was a latter-day Marconi and was inordinately proud of my expertise. I had grown to relish the broadcasts my family would listen to in our New York City apartment, so that when we returned to the country I felt deprived and longed to tune in. The signals were there on the airwaves, but we had no receiver. One partly successful effort on my part had been to get a rudimentary crystal set at the five-and-ten-cent store. This basically consisted of a pair of earphones and the rectifying device of a galena crystal. One would move a small wire called a cat's whisker to various parts of the crystal and sometimes a subliminally faint signal would come in. The first of my crystal-radio receptions happened to be "The Chase and Sanborn Hour" (advertising coffee), in which the Sherlock Holmes story "The Musgrave Ritual" was aired. Success was thrilling but limited—too faint to rely on for anything but entertainment by good luck.

While I was at school, Mr. Fair arranged for a carpenter to come and teach "manual arts." He arrived in the basement with his tools, some two-by-fours, and a few pieces of wood of other dimensions. We watched him saw and trim and nail, and by the time he was finished he had made and outfitted a carpenter's workshop. I never forgot the spectacle of his carpentry skills. It was thrilling to watch him assemble the workbench that we would be working on. His steady purposefulness, his judgment, his unhurried handiwork were a lesson in itself. In that basement we made magazine racks for our parents. Some showed great skill, the wood beautifully stained. My contribution didn't seem to come together; a kind of entropy set in to defeat my carpentry. But with a few deft strokes by our instructor, the magazine rack was given back the status of a useful piece of furniture. I came home proud of having made something, which my mother kept as a treasured piece. A school today would probably order a workbench from somewhere in Vermont, and the best part of the course would be skipped.

One skill that I have especially enjoyed and that has proved useful in my work as a publisher is photography. I remember seeing my first camera under the pine tree when I received it at some Christmas in the 1920s. It was love at first sight, but the real excitement came when I took my first pictures of my grandmother's garden in Morristown, New Jersey. She had built there a lovely little open-air chapel, and yours truly was commissioned to photograph it with my new camera. My sister Julia stood on the chapel steps to create the impression of a bustling congregation. A week or so later, when the film had been developed, printed, and returned, I couldn't believe that anything in the graphic arts field could be so exquisitely beautiful. All photographs were then black and white, but it was possible to tint them with special watercolors. My mother and sister and I together colored them, adding special vividness by applying golden, ecclesiastical hues to appropriate parts of the building. As a boy photographer, I was somewhat short on subjects. When I look at the albums enshrining my work, it turns out to consist of two kinds of portraits: all the members of the family wearing self-conscious expressions and hundreds of pictures of cats, kittens, cows, and sheep in passive and vaguely picturesque poses. Such was the beginning of a lifelong career of taking pictures.

I can still feel in my bones the dramatic sequence required by a Brownie camera. You framed your picture on a little ground-glass pane, holding the box as straight and steady as you could, and then gently pulled the shutter until it snapped. It was a thrilling business, because though you increased the pressure on the lever, nothing happened to the shutter until it gave a brisk click. You knew how much film was left as you turned the little crank because the number of each frame appeared behind the small red hole at the back of the box. The film would be dropped off at the drugstore, and you had to wait a week or so for the roll to be processed. In my memories photographs are always associated with the symphony of smells at the drugstore—the mysterious sweet odor of the raw film before it was processed and the rather tangy odor of the finished snapshots. Opening the red and yellow envelopes in which they were returned was suspenseful; sometimes on several negatives nothing came out at all, because of some technical error on the part of the photographer. Sometimes, while the pictures came out well enough, they had to be turned 180 degrees to be right side up.

In those days improvements were made almost every year in the chemistry of the film emulsion. Most of these improvements were made by the Eastman Kodak Company, which would promote them with a barrage of Latin and Greek trade names. As I remember, things started with orthochromatic film. It failed to capture more background than the white light of the sky, not registering the reds at all. Orthochromatic—literally "correct color"—graduated to panchromatic, which means "all colors" and which prevailed until around the time of World War II, when Kodachrome and Ektachrome film then replaced black and white.

The lens of the Brownie camera was scarcely visible from the outside; one didn't think about the lens because it was an integral part of the box itself. Not until the smaller cameras were designed did the lens come into its own as the crucial element in photography, and being various for various purposes added considerably to the expense of the equipment. It's strange to realize now that the simplest lens can consist of letting the light shine through a pinhole. A lens of glass only modifies in one way or another the optical fact of using light to perform a chemical operation on film. I recall seeing a collection of photographs taken by a renowned photographer who had used nothing but a pinhole as a lens to show what he could do. Everyone marveled at the beauty of the works thus achieved. Nothing could have been more at odds with the progress of photography, in which more and more expensive lenses were produced, with the attention being placed on technology at the expense of technique and composition, though only the latter produce pictures as works of art.

As an adult I would process the film myself, sometimes experimenting with green or blue dyes, with results that were spectacular but not very realistic. My darkroom was the bathroom serving on a part-time basis, with the enlarger sitting on the commode and the wet films dangling from the shower rod. Developing prints was of course another joy added to the rest. Watching an exposed enlargement come to life as it is submerged in the developer is one of the most dramatic chemical miracles science has produced. This early knowledge of photography enabled me as a publisher to take a special interest in designing and producing the jackets and illustrations for Scribner books.

Harking back to "the uncommitted cortex," I am impressed by the facility it lends to learning at an early age. Children in their teens gradually lose some of the learning capacity of their childhood, but that loss is offset by the greater depth of feeling and enthusiasm that follows physical maturity. And this in turn often leads—as it did in my case—to a lifelong commitment to learning.

Afterthoughts

❧

Looking back over my life, I am conscious that some of my happiest moments were spent with my family. One summer when the children were very young, Joan and I rented a house in Darien, Connecticut, not far from the railway station. Each evening, returning from New York, I would walk up the pebbly dirt driveway and see my eldest son, Charlie, then about four years old, running down to meet me. Occasionally he'd trip and fall, get up, and start running again to greet his father. By some gift of prophecy, I would say to myself, "This is one of the happiest experiences I'll ever have in my life"—as indeed it was.

Several family outings particularly stand out. One of the most memorable was a motor trip in 1970 to Sea Island, an ocean resort in southern Georgia. We traveled in a Ford Falcon station wagon, the best car we ever owned. Each member of the family laid claim to a particular place in the car. I drove, with Joan beside me. Charlie and Blair, aged eighteen and fifteen, rode in the back seat, and my youngest son, John, age twelve, made a kind of nest for himself in the very back of the car, surrounded by comic books and virtually never coming up for air. The trip took two days of driving; today it would be shorter thanks to interstate highways. We were not very far out of New York—or so it seemed—when we saw the first sign showing how many miles it was to "Pedro's" and for the remainder of the trip we were kept apprised of how close we were getting—or how far away we were, once we had passed Pedro's "South of the Border" lodge in South Carolina. The children loved these statistics, and soon every other remark in our conversation was: "How close are we to 'Pedro's'?" The children were fascinated by this well-advertised roadside stop and restaurant, after which they were later awestruck by its huge display of fireworks; they would have been illegal in New Jersey, and the Scribner household as well! By the time we had blinked and gazed at the fireworks, it was time to turn in. To our surprise, we found a dining room that served a scrumptious filet mignon; all we had been prepared for was hot dogs and hamburgers.

There was a great deal of singing in the car, and games, in addition to keeping track of the mileage, and occasional pit stops for ice cream cones and bona-fide meals. What fun those trips were! Aiming to make things as democratic as possible, I tried to blur the age difference between parents and children; it seemed to give way when we were all members of an expedition. Children deserve such periods in which all differences are dissolved into a common status. It's not as easy to do that at home, because there are too many tiresome tasks to fulfill. On a trip, these responsibilities can be taken with an intentional insouciance. I would relish being able to repeat one of these trips now, but I'd have to recruit a couple of grandchildren for the purpose!

I could recite other fond memories that are intertwined with my intellectual and professional recollections, but they had best remain private. A far more disturbing remembrance takes me back to a vacation in Maine in the mid 1980s when I was struck by what I thought was a visual disorder—one that was extremely difficult to pin down. The first symptom appeared as I drove up from New Jersey. I had always thought of myself as an extremely cautious driver, and I was horrified when Joan told me that I was failing to stay in my lane on the highway. I had no inkling that I was driving outside the line and was frankly puzzled and—dare I say?—slightly annoyed at what I thought was backseat driving. Shortly afterwards, when I had to drive through an underpass with trucks to the left and cars to the right, I felt alarmingly bewildered in trying to navigate the road. I complained about how badly the truckers were driving these days—they seemed to be driving me off the road. After a close encounter with a truck barreling down on top of us, I then and there decided that I would not attempt to drive at all until I knew whether I was suffering a one-time predicament or something chronic. I still thought my difficulty was due to the truck driver's recklessness. Even so, I was full of anxiety whenever I was in the car and was losing assurance in my ability to drive.

One eye doctor I went to see advised me to make sure that my glasses were clean; another assured me that I needed a cataract operation, which, I was told, would be simple and safe. On the principle of postponing surgery until a second opinion confirmed the need, I went to an ophthalmologist, who doubted that I had any cataracts at all; in fact, he said he would go on the theory that I had not and scheduled a visual field test. I thought things were going famously, that I might even set a record for outstanding visual acuity, when to my horror the doctor interpreting said, "There's nothing wrong with your eyes, but the evidence points to a serious neurological problem—possibly a silent stroke." He showed me an inked page that seemed about ninety-five percent black and five percent white. I said, "Is the black good or bad?" He said "bad." The page began to look to me like a skull and crossbones.

I made an appointment at New York Hospital and was examined by a leading neurologist, Dr. John Coronna. He seemed extremely concerned and asked his nurse to arrange a CAT scan *"immediatement!"* His use of the French word frightened me more than anything else—it emphasized his concern. As I gathered later, he wanted to see if there was any evidence of a stroke or other brain damage. The tests came back showing, much to our relief, no evidence of a brain tumor or stroke. The status of my problem was undetermined, with no one able to put a name to it. A series of psychological tests was administered to assess my ability to read, to remember passages that had been spoken, and to identify faces. For a good while the problem remained a mystery. Finally, a second neurologist, Dr. Mark Tramo, said that they had finally been able to solve it: I suffered from a hitherto unfamiliar trouble known as the Holmes syndrome. The technical description is *spatial, visual, simul agnosia*. It had been first diagnosed during World War I by a Dr. Holmes who specialized in the surgery of cranial injuries. I did not relish the diagnosis; I did not remember having fallen off a horse or doing anything that could have caused a brain injury. But there didn't seem to be any course of action to take, except to rule out other possibilities.

It was indeed suggested that I take some pills to help the visual difficulties created by a brain abnormality. One of the doctors mentioned a medicine that had been effective in treating the symptoms of Alzheimer's disease. I said to the doctor in a restrained way that I rather wished he had not mentioned *that* possibility. He quickly reassured me: Alzheimer's was a global disease of the brain, whereas mine was the localized degeneration of a nerve cell. Contemporaneous with these discussions and tests was a kind of "council of war" as to what we should do next. The neurologists felt that nothing could be hoped for in the way of a cure or total correction of the difficulty. I would just have to learn to live with it.

First of all, driving a car was totally verboten. Because of the difficulty I would have in tying shoes, pouring liquids, and so on, it was suggested that I have a valet. Despite the swanky sound of the word, it chilled my blood to think of a stranger around me to help with the simple tasks of everyday life. Since I have an incredibly patient wife in Joan, we decided to put the valet idea on the bottom shelf and see how we could get by without outside help. Throughout Joan had been—and remains—uncomplaining, although the multiple difficulties that arise daily are both trying and tiresome.

Obviously reading, writing, and editing were seriously affected. At work, when a word had to be interpolated in the middle of a sentence, I had a hard time locating the exact spot. My reading degenerated rather rapidly. As I read a paragraph or went from one page to another, I invariably lost my place and had to backtrack. These inaccuracies became so frequent that reading soon became extremely taxing—and writing as well. Although in the past my writing could turn sloppy under pressure, now everything I wrote came out undecipherable of its own accord.

It was clear that the Holmes syndrome was rare and little known, so medical students were eager to work on my case. Besides, it seemed a good opportunity to understand normal visual processes by studying an abnormal one. I frequently met with these students of neuropsychology, both for the sake of scientific understanding and animated in the hope that they might ultimately have good news for me.

At this point it was suggested that occupational therapy might make everyday life much easier. A young expert in that field, Joan Toglia, volunteered to take on my case, and her positive attitude—her conviction that she could help—was the beginning of a relearning process that has continued for a good long time. Over the years she invented various strategies to help me cope with everyday activities—writing a check, looking up a number in the telephone book, and verifying simple arithmetic. Miss Toglia was tireless in her efforts, and as a result of the confidence she induced, my morale began to soar and my everyday life came closer to normal than was earlier thought possible.

Knowing that reading books had been not only an integral part of my profession but, indeed, a fundamental part of my daily life, a number of friends brought to my attention the availability of books recorded on cassette tapes. These friends told me how much pleasure they got from listening to these recordings and urged me to follow their example. It seems somewhat contradictory at first that a man who has always advocated printed books over audiovisual devices should now be confined through sheer necessity to listening to books on tape. Nevertheless, I have found some of the recordings extremely literate and have savored some of the dramatic readings made by some of the recorders. Given my choice, I'd still rather read and see the printed word, reserving books on tape for times when one cannot physically read a book but would still like to enjoy a literary work—such as on automobile trips.

Several firms issue these tapes. Recorded Books and Books on Tape are notable "publishers" of them and offer a broad repertory of fiction and nonfiction, classics, and popular titles. The borrower can rent the works for thirty days at a reasonable fee. Another important source of recorded reading for handicapped readers is the Library of Congress series called Talking Books. They are more scholarly and varied, and among them are marvelous books on science, history, and literature. Talking Books works as a lending library for certified visually impaired readers, and the service is free of charge.

It never dawned on me that these spoken books would become a major part of my intellectual life and recreational reading. By now I must have "read" hundreds of books in this way. I was never a rapid reader as a boy, although my retention was high. Paradoxically, now that I was reading books on tape, my reading speed was better than ever and my retention just as good. I can fairly say that for me the discovery of this mode of reading was a kind of "open sesame" to my continued enjoyment of literature.

A few years ago, after the onset of my disability, I wrote a book about my career as a publisher, *In the Company of Writers*. It pleased me greatly to find it later recorded by Books on Tape. We are told that "the Lord giveth and the Lord taketh away." I have been deprived but I have been compensated through the intellectual joys of this new avenue of reading.

While pursuing my literary and scientific interests, I did not abandon essay writing and other literary work. This was made possible by the help of a young assistant, Lisa Griffith, who wrote down what I composed in my mind—a letter, a story, a memoir. I had never composed in this fashion before, and it was my good fortune to find I could do it with almost as much ease as with pencil and paper. I learned to dictate with enough facility to write more than eighty columns for a weekly newspaper of Malcolm Forbes's in New Jersey, handle all my corre-

spondence, and do other writing, such as this very book.*
Perhaps it's another instance of a handicap honing a skill.
Another triumph of occupational therapy was that it taught me
to write a legible signature I could repeat as many times as
necessary—helpful in signing the flyleaf of 3,000 books.

---

*In the pages that follow are a sampling of columns I wrote, under the title
"Afterthoughts" for Malcolm's newspaper that family and close friends claim to have
found entertaining. It is with some temerity that I have been persuaded to include
them as an Appendix to this work.

Appendices

Appendix A

Columns for Malcolm

Breaking into Print

So often when I tell someone that I'm a book publisher they ask "What do you have to do to get a book published?" Of course one of the first things I ask them is whether they've written a book or whether they're just thinking of writing one, and I have to explain that there's really not much advice for me to give until they're beyond the stage of thinking about it.

In studying the careers of many of the world's famous authors it is interesting to note how many of them have had rather similar experiences in breaking into print for the first time. So often the nest egg for their first book consists of writing that has no initial promise of being a great work of literature. For example, the novelist Tolstoy was a soldier in the czar's army. An avid reader, he read a Russian translation of Dickens's *David Copperfield* and was so enamored with the story that it motivated him to write a novel based on his own Russian boyhood. Later, having submitted his work to a literary magazine and having it accepted, he started his career with a momentum that never abated. Although one would not think so without knowing the facts, Dickens was a great inspiration to Russian writers including Tolstoy's contemporary, Fyodor Dostoyevski. That raises the question how Dickens himself got started as a novelist. As is now well-known, he served for a time as a kind of political reporter, an occupation that motivated him to learn shorthand as well as write down his thoughts with great speed. In the course of time he began to compose poignant and amusing little sketches of London life, a collection of which constituted his first book, *Sketches by Boz*, all of which were published first in newspaper form and which made him a comparatively well-known imaginative journalist. One day a printseller who had collected a series of popular sporting illustrations asked him if he would write a series of captions to go with the various prints. Dickens accepted this commission, but instead of producing individual captions, he found himself embarking on a serial narrative that became one of the greatest of all novels: *The Pickwick Papers*.

It is remarkable how many novelists began their careers as journalists. In addition to Dickens, we can think of Mark Twain, Herman Melville, and Ernest Hemingway. I think the comparative ease of putting words on paper in a "journalistic spirit" serves to reduce some of the anxiety and lack of a subject that inhibit so many would-be novelists.

Confessions of a Mongoose Lover

I realize that it is bordering on sacrilege to raise questions about the handiwork of the Creator, but I have often thought that if I were responsible for producing life on earth, I would not have included snakes in the agenda. It's pretty clear that the Creator had some afterthoughts on that subject since the serpent in the Garden of Eden caused a good deal of unnecessary trouble. The serpent was duly punished, and Adam and his wife were banned from the garden and left to fend for themselves. Here again, I have a possibly tactless comment to make. Speaking for myself, I would much prefer to produce my food by the sweat of my brow than to live for eternity in a garden with a talking snake.

The Greeks had a word for it—*herpetophobia*—which means a dread of snakes. I can remember quite clearly seeing my first snake at the Old Stone House in New Jersey where our family's cook, who was Irish and had no prior experience with snakes (since Saint Patrick had banished them from Ireland), was taken by a fit of hysterics when a rather tiny white snake slithered back down its hole with a motion that is still able to upset me as I recall it. My mother, who was an intrepid horsewoman and far beyond fearing a lowly garter snake, thought that her son might benefit from a trip to the Snake House in the Bronx Zoo. An appointment was made with the keeper for that purpose, and my sister and I stood by while one or two men brought out a yard or so of boa constrictor stretched full-length and regarding us with a beady eye. It was apparent that I wanted to get away from its gaze as far and as quickly as possible, but one more effort was made to convince me that the king snake my mother was holding was not clammy in texture or in any respect an object of fear. In fact, she went so far as to come close to draping it around my neck, at which point I immediately lost consciousness.

Since that abortive attempt to free me from herpetophobia, the fear of snakes of whatever size or color has been a trial to me and in some respects influenced my life. When World War II was declared, many American servicemen were assigned to war games in the deep South, and I remember reading a terrifying newspaper report of one or more GIs jumping into foxholes tenanted at the time by rattlesnakes. It was at that moment that my decision to sign up for the U.S. Navy was cast in concrete. I am willing to give my life for my country, but not if it involves consorting with snakes. I now realize that most people, regardless of sex, suffer from herpetophobia, although not all are quite as cowardly as I am in that respect. I remember once watching a golf playoff between Jack Nicklaus and Lee Trevino in which Trevino threw a most convincing green rubber snake on the grass just as Nicklaus was teeing off. In my mind such a prank was clear grounds for forfeiting the tournament, but Nicklaus took it in good grace and went on to win. One more example of his courage and sportsmanship.

Another experience that might have freed me from fear of snakes but had entirely the opposite effect was a trip to the Grand Canyon, which appears to be something of a resort area for rattlesnakes. On the way down the trail, one of my companions let out a shout, saying, "Look at the snake!" Like a fool, I leaned over to where the snake was—it was in a kind of drainage ditch—and found myself gazing eye-to-eye with a rattler. I then took what soldiers call "evasive action" and ran as far as I could up the trail. But I was not yet free from the menace, since it was necessary to walk through a kind of tunnel built for the purpose of crossing to the other side of the Colorado River. Since this was obviously an area in which snakes might be expected to infest as a way of getting out of the sun, I had to walk a good many yards listening to the sound of plant pods rattling in the wind as I wondered whether some of them might be the real thing.

That was the end of my Grand Canyon experiences, but as a publisher I have often had to read manuscripts filled with upsetting snake descriptions. We had an author named Elliot Chaze who managed to put at least one rattlesnake in each of his books. I questioned him about that propensity since it had become clear to me that he was as much a coward on that score as I was. "It's very simple," he said. "If I am writing part of a novel and my attention begins to lag, I bring a snake into the story and that wakes me up right away and helps me focus on what's taking place." I found it also worked for me to focus on what he was writing. After comparing notes on this fairly cowardly phobia shared by us both, it was decided that we might found the Herpetophobia Society of the United States and publish a journal for fellow sufferers. Perhaps we might even bring Indiana Jones into the organization as our Hollywood representative. Whatever happens, I will be sure to keep you informed!

Does Music Teach You Music?

My first exposure to classical music was at St. Paul's School. The library had some records available on a rotating loan basis. Without knowing anything about Beethoven, I borrowed his Sixth Symphony, known as the Pastoral Symphony. For a blind choice it was a marvelously lucky one because I can't think of any of his music that is more accessible to a beginner than that one. It's got so many wonderful programmatic passages, including a kind of peasant outing or picnic, plus a rather convincing thunderstorm. In those days we weren't terribly venturesome, musically speaking. Most of us were intoxicated by Tchaikovsky's great symphonies until we were virtually exhausted by the passionate outpouring of that great Russian composer.

When one is listening to familiar music, one often anticipates what will happen next in the composition. I'm sure many of my readers have had the experience of hearing with one's inner ear what will happen next. It's a good sign. It shows that the music is really entering your mind and establishing itself there. In fact, I am sure that this anticipation becomes part of the musical experience and has a great deal to do with one's pleasure. It isn't just accidental that first movements contain a long repeat da capo. That is the player's way of making sure that you will not be deprived of the anticipation. It is that familiarity that makes it part of you—a whole line of music has engraved itself on your mind.

There is another element in the enjoyment of listening to music and that is the fact that music seems to be pushing one to higher levels of sophistication that one could not have anticipated. It was a chance remark of a friend that brought Schubert into my musical life and opened up for me his marvelous compositions. In my schoolboy years, there were so many discoveries to be made. One of the most important was the discovery of Beethoven's symphonies, and I still believe that getting to know his nine symphonies is as important as knowing the plays of Shakespeare.

In those earlier years there were no compact discs. So many of the great recordings, such as those by Columbia, had to be acquired in their familiar green jackets pound by pound. It was almost impossible to carry more than a few of them at one time. So many of the things that we enjoyed would now be considered potboilers. We fussed an awful lot with needles. One time before the diamond and other jewel-like needles were developed, we experimented with cactus thorns, sharpened by little twirling pieces of sandpaper.

There is another curious phenomenon of listening to classical music that I'm sure we all experience—namely, that the first recordings we hear and get to know seem to imprint themselves in a way that other later renditions don't entirely match. They tell me that songbirds are imprinted this way in the nest and never forget their melodies. Most of the Beethoven works I learned were performed under the direction of the great conductor Felix Weingartner, and any other performance, however marvelous it may be, still doesn't seem exactly correct. I was in a room in boarding school with a fairly potent homemade phonograph system, and I remember one night after I'd been playing music, an older teacher on the floor above told me that he had heard me playing Beethoven's Seventh Symphony and he had lain down and put his ear to the floor so that he wouldn't miss the cello variations in the third movement, a comment that left an indelible mark on me.

Thoughts in a Transcontinental Roomette

Many years ago, returning by train from a publishing trip in San Francisco, I found myself sitting in a roomette looking out on what must have been the bleakest desert terrain that our country can display. Mile after mile sped by with virtually nothing to arrest one's interest or stimulate one's imagination. As always happens on a train, you hear the clicking of the cars beating out a refrain that no amount of effort can completely silence. In some strange mental preoccupation, I found myself meditating on the concept of beauty as we perceive it. Perhaps it was the absence of beauty seen through the window that steered me in that direction, and my thoughts turned at once to flowers.

Almost everyone is enchanted by the beauty of flowers, but I wonder if our reaction to such beauty can be explained. At least as a preliminary approach, it strikes me that there are two aspects in the design of most flowers that our mind perceives and appreciates. The first is what I would tentatively describe as the formal beauty of the flower—its geometrical elegance repeating itself constantly with a precision that charms us. Some of its forms are clearly geometrical, and our eyes see them as such. But at the same time, we are also keenly aware of the spontaneous, almost vivacious aspect of the flower as a living creation of nature. Each of these aspects we can focus on separately, but the full joy that the flower gives us is the combination of the two. One part of our mind is touched by the formal elegance while another part is thrilled by the imaginative variations. It seems almost unnecessary to point out that mankind has been tutored in beauty by nature itself and that mankind's efforts to produce such beauty in virtually all forms of art reflects many of the devices of nature's artistic expedience in combining elements that suggest an almost mathematical structure with the spontaneity of life itself. Nature abhors total monotony as much as we do.

You cannot go to a gallery of sculpture or painting, or listen to a concert, or read a poem, without appreciating how art speaks to the two aspects of beauty that I have described. Similarly, when we see some of the early hand-crafted products of the past they are much more pleasing to us than the mindless repetitions and perfect geometrical productions of the machine age. For example, we see in a hand-carved newel post of a staircase something far more charming than in a perfectly shaped machine-made product. This is partly because the handmade object gives us a sense of the actual struggle of the craftsman imposing his form on the material, which in our mind conveys a sense of the life and art of the person who created it.

No composer worthy of the name allows his music to become exactly predictable and no poet would allow his metrical system to be so either. But every work of art has to be at least in part predictable to tame its elements into the formal organization that our mind can perceive, accept, and enjoy.

In the Web of Ideas

How to Cook a Kangaroo

Several years ago I attended a lecture at the Museum of Natural History in New York by the anthropologist Stephen Jay Gould, who had studied the life of an extremely primitive Australian tribe, the Yawara. These people were eking out an existence against difficulties in which none of us could survive. The desert was fiercely hot during the day, but at night the tribe's people had to huddle together nakedly with no protection from the cold. Their main source of meat came from slaying kangaroos, which they roasted by digging a pit and lowering the dead kangaroo, in a sitting position, into a bed of glowing coals. At this point in the lecture I had a bright idea, and during the question period I asked Dr. Gould why they didn't skin the kangaroo before roasting it, and use its hide as a protection from the cold. Dr. Gould was quite definite in his answer. The Yawara would understand exactly this idea, but to them it had one fatal drawback: that just wasn't the proper way to cook a kangaroo.

I've thought of the Yawara and their hide-bound conservatism many times since that lecture and have wondered about some of our own customs. They think of us as rootless because we have no real ties to the land that approach theirs, and they think of us as helpless because we could not survive for twenty-four hours in the desert in which they spend their whole lives. Their sense of knowing where they are at all times is absolutely uncanny and may be enhanced by the fact that they view the rocks themselves as their ancestors.

It's easy to patronize these primitive tribesmen, but before we become too critical, perhaps we might consider the fact that generations from now mankind may view some of our pet customs as being just as foolish, just as inhumane, and just as superstitious as the customs of the Yawara. To our descendants a few centuries from now we may seem absurdly backward when it comes to "cooking our own kangaroo."

Mental Photography

On a 1989 visit to Northeast Harbor, Maine, I had the opportunity to see three of the most beautiful gardens on the East Coast: the Thuya Gardens, the Abbey Rockefeller Garden, and the Meditation Garden at the Asticou Inn. As a lifelong shutterbug, I found myself at a loss by not having a camera. Then it occurred to me that a reasonable substitute might be to commit each of these gardens to memory as well as I could. The procedure was very simple. I would look very intently at a particular flower bed or tree or path, checking the impression of each by opening and closing my eyes to see how well my mind had captured them. To my surprise this was a great deal easier than I had anticipated. It did not seem difficult to fix pretty accurate images, even including some of the bees and other insects involved in the same pursuit. What a joy it was to realize that I was capturing the delightful images well enough to enjoy them when I returned home. Indeed that is just what happened. During the following year, I had the pleasure of revisiting these gardens with my mind's eye and with the added satisfaction that this had required no tripods, no light meters, no film, and no albums!

A Date with a Gorilla

In the seventies my wife Joan and I flew to San Francisco on a publishing trip. On the day we left there was an article in the *New York Times* describing the project of a young graduate student at Stanford to communicate verbally with a young female gorilla named KoKo. This project was based on the idea that the gorilla had no faculties for speech but might have an ability to speak and even think in sign language.

I was fascinated by this idea and called Penny Patterson, KoKo's trainer, to see if I could have an opportunity to see how this project was developing. Because of my connections with the media, she did arrange for our paying a visit in Palo Alto where she and her charge were living in a trailer that contained a fairly large cage for KoKo. As my introduction to KoKo, who was standing nearby inside the cage, the gorilla crossed her arms to her chest and then pointed both hands to me, indicating that she loved me (at first sight). I reciprocated the gesture. After that, she played like a little child, pushing a small Mickey Mouse doll through the bars and then asking me to blow on it. A boyfriend of Penny's who was there at the time, looking wistful if not glum, said to me, "KoKo doesn't care about the Mickey Mouse doll, she just wants to make a fool of you." To which I responded that that has happened to me many times in my life, but this was the first of its kind.

Everything KoKo did was written down in a notebook by Miss Patterson, and it was marvelous to see the parental pride and concern that she had for her charge. Later we learned that KoKo liked men better than women, which she demonstrated by making a terrifyingly violent lunge at Joan, who was fortunately protected by the grating but unable to quell a cry of sheer terror. This animal struck me more and more as a teasing, unruly child. If Miss Patterson put a tiny rubber crocodile through the cage, KoKo would hide her head and run back and forth screaming with alarm just as a child might.

Later in the afternoon, three deaf-mutes drove up in their Volkswagen to see if they could communicate, and Miss Patterson brought KoKo out for a little recreation. First she jumped onto a tree, shaking all the branches in a kind of frenzy, and later jumped on top of the Volkswagen and beat furiously on the lid with her paws, a development that caused some concern for the visitors, as one might understand. The thing that struck me the most was when she climbed up on top of the barbed wire surrounding the trailer and was able to run up and down and back and forth with an agility that no human could ever duplicate.

From time to time I would read something in the papers about the attempts to communicate with KoKo, but as far as I remember no really positive results were achieved by anyone. I'm not surprised, because I believe so strongly that between humans and animals there is a chasm that will never be bridged. It may be kinder to the animals themselves that this separation is fundamental and ineradicable.

Stepping into Humanness

Every day thousands of infants are taking their first steps under the admiring eyes of their mothers and fathers. There's an old saying—"Walk at one, talk at two"—but clearly the most important of these two skills is the latter one, in which the child says his first words by design rather than chance. So until that step is taken, the child is properly referred to as an infant, from the Latin word *infans* meaning "not speaking."

Taking this tentative step from infancy to speech, the child is bridging the entire chasm that separates animals and human beings. In fact, I would go so far as to say that our ability to think and communicate in this way represents the greatest evolutionary stride in all of nature, and is the most fundamental and most fruitful of all changes in the life of a child.

Children learning to speak and understand the meaning of words very rapidly become more and more adept in learning, to a degree that one could consider this achievement of speech as one of the virtuoso performances of human maturity. The scientific literature on this subject is rich and absorbing. For example, some children have learned to play chess simply by watching the moves of a player, but their skills in handling words and sentences are nothing short of breathtaking. Children in families of mixed languages are able to speak with accuracy in more than two languages, shifting from one to another with apparent ease. In view of these marvelous and seemingly miraculous achievements of children, isn't it appropriate to consider what they are taught and what they learn as one of the major responsibilities for the future of each child?

It's easy for us to have a demonstration of the power of speech when we observe that we have no retrievable memory before the age at which we learned to speak. In other words, it is speech that provides the basis for the production of retrievable memory. I say *retrievable* because a child may maintain fears or shocks sustained in his or her infancy, but as a kind of brute memory only.

Not only is this power of speech essential to communication, but speech and words are probably the elements through which we can summon experiences of our own past. Our minds are structured and empowered by this capacity to speak. The words we have acquired provide the mechanism of marking these experiences for later retrieval. If we want to retrieve an idea, it is through words, even though this may take place unconsciously. We possess the great power of bringing things into our minds at will—by tagging thoughts with words.

If I want to say to myself, "When I go downstairs, I'm going to take the Lexington Avenue Subway," what makes possible that rehearsal is the power of speech. I can pull it out of my earlier experience with retrievable memory. I asked Jim Luce, professor of classics at Princeton, if the Greeks had a word for "wordmaker," because I thought that this word making and word using was the essential gift of our humanness. He told me that he knew of no such word, but pointed out that the Greek playwright, Sophocles, considered the invention of speech one of the greatest gifts to mankind by the god Dionysus.

The more we find out about our power of speech, the more we'll understand what we've been given by this power. Speech has created and shaped our minds, and made possible all the benefits of our humanness.

Appendix B

A Family Tradition

Reprinted below is my brief history of Charles Scribner's Sons, published in 1957 in the American Library Association *Bulletin*. A far more detailed account of my own four decades at the house is found in my 1990 memoir, *In the Company of Writers*. In 1984 Scribners merged into the Macmillan Publishing Company, where today our reference, juvenile, and adult trade imprints continue to flourish.

The history of Charles Scribner's Sons begins with the publishing partnership of Isaac D. Baker and Charles Scribner established in 1846. The second partner, Scribner, was a young New Yorker of twenty-five who had not long before graduated from Princeton (class of 1840). He had first planned on a career in the law but because of poor health had had to give that up for something less strenuous and turned to publishing as more congenial. (It would be interesting to find out if the relative hardship of the two occupations would still be settled in the same way.) The location picked for the new firm was part of the Brick Meeting House on the corner of Nassau Street and Park

Row, in an area of lower Manhattan that was then a kind of headquarters of the book trade.

At that time to start an independent book-publishing company was something of an innovation, for most of the established houses had grown out of printing businesses or bookselling. There were, however, real advantages in this situation, particularly insofar as the firm was able to begin business without having to worry about keeping a manufacturing plant busy at all costs. It made it possible for them to stick to the work of new authors, particularly American authors, without attempting to compete in publishing reprints of the various established writers, Scott, for example, or Macaulay, or the English poets. In short, the firm set out to originate works and to discover fresh talent. It's still a good policy.

According to modern tastes not all of the first titles of Baker and Scribner would make very entertaining reading. Theological treatises were numerous, many of them almost impenetrable today. It is believed that actually the first work to be published was an austere tome entitled *The Puritans and Their Principles*, by Edwin Hall. How uncomfortably would that book stand on a shelf beside some of our later-day best-sellers.

Nothing does quite as much for a publishing business as a best-seller. It is probable that the long life of this firm is owed at least in part to the big sale in the very beginning of a book entitled *Napoleon and His Marshals* by the Reverend J. T. Headley. From all accounts it was far from being a model of historical accuracy, but then how many best-sellers are?

There were also the familiar (and more trying) cases where the first book or books of an author were disappointments. For instance, there was Donald G. Mitchell, or "Ik Marvel," who came to the firm after one nonbest-seller at another house. The partners decided to invest in his talent, but the second book, *Battle Summer* (1849), failed too. *Reveries of a Bachelor*, published the next year, caught on, however, and the hoped-for success was won in spades. From then on Ik Marvel was a "name author." A few years ago when we were moving things around in our printing plant, the Scribner Press, we came upon an antique box containing the printing plates of *Reveries of a Bachelor*. It is difficult to say for how many decades these had escaped melting—perhaps through a series of oversights, perhaps because of the sure respect of publishers for a best-seller—even last century's.

Baker died in 1850, and the management devolved upon Charles Scribner alone. It was a period of growth, and there were projects that undoubtedly did much to put the new firm on the map. Over the years it had been building up a fine list of books on religion. This program reached a high point around the time of the Civil War, when Scribner set out to publish an American version of the mammoth work of German biblical scholarship, Lange's *Biblical Commentary*. Eventually completed in twenty-six large volumes (financed at enormous cost), the set was a commercial and critical success. It was copublished in Britain by Clark of Edinburgh—something of a feather in the cap of the American firm, for Clark had himself begun a translation of Lange that he dropped in favor of ours. Publishing ties are often very old, and it is interesting to note here that Scribners is currently at work with T. & T. Clark of Edinburgh on a revision of Hasting's *Dictionary of the Bible* — almost a hundred years later. Religious books are still a strong part of our list.

In 1865 Charles Scribner and Company took its first step in magazine publishing with the somewhat staid *Hours at Home*. Although this was apparently successful, plans were soon made for transforming it into something much more ambitious. In 1870 a new firm, Scribner & Co., was formed to bring out an enlarged successor with the name *Scribner's Monthly: An*

Illustrated Magazine for the People. The magazine thrived and was soon strong enough to start encouraging young American writers. But Charles Scribner did not live to see its growth and success, for he died of typhoid the next year (1871) on a trip abroad. Behind him in the firm he left his eldest son, John Blair Scribner, and on this young man (he was only twenty at the time) fell the job of carrying on the family interests in the business.

This was by no means a period of marking time. In two years (1873) Scribner & Co., launched the famous children's magazine *St. Nicholas* under the editorship of Mary Mapes Dodge, with Frank R. Stockton as assistant editor. This connection was later to bring many fine books to the publishing firm and establish them permanently in the field of children's literature. There was, for example, an edition of Mary Mapes Dodge's own *Hans Brinker and the Silver Skates* (1876), a book that is selling strongly on our list today. In a different vein was *The American Boy's Handy Book* (1882), by the truly immortal Dan Beard. We still get letters addressed to him.

A second important development of these years was the coming of age of the Subscription Book Department, which began to undertake some very big things. In association with Messrs. Black of Edinburgh it brought out an American edition of the *Encyclopaedia Britannica* (9th ed.), of which it sold some seventy thousand sets (four times as many as were sold in Britian). In those days, as well as now, businessmen liked to play up the size of large numbers by various imaginary calculations. Thus it was asserted that all those volumes of the *Encyclopaedia* if laid end to end would have reached "from New York beyond Omaha." An inspiring thought.

In later years the Subscription Book Department published library sets of the works of such well-known authors as Rudyard Kipling, Robert Louis Stevenson, Henry James, and

James M. Barrie (to name a few). It is just as active now (some eighty years later) in the distribution of the *Dictionary of American Biography*, the *Dictionary of American History*, and several other established sets and reference works.

But let us return to the 1870s, for that was a critical period. In 1875 Charles Scribner II graduated from Princeton and at once joined his brother John Blair in the business. There were two other partners at the time: Edward Seymour and Andrew C. Armstrong, but Seymour died in 1877, and the next year Armstrong sold the Scribners his share, intending to start up his own concern. This left the main book-publishing company wholly owned and controlled by the Scribner family. The name was now changed to Charles Scribner's Sons, which the firm has retained ever since. In the next year (1879), however, John Blair Scribner died, leaving Charles II (who was then twenty-five) to manage the business alone. At first he was to have his hands full.

For one thing, all was not harmonious at the magazine firm, Scribner & Co. The other owners of that concern chafed at being in any way beholden to Charles Scribner's Sons. There was talk of their publishing books themselves, and probably each side regarded the other as the tail trying to wag the dog. When, in 1881, one of the partners, Roswell Smith, bought up enough stock to acquire individual control, the equilibrium was disturbed, to put it mildly. Only a few months later CS II, refusing (as he said) to retain a minority interest, sold to Smith all the Charles Scribner's Sons stock in Scribner & Co.

Thus *Scribner's Monthly* and *St. Nicholas* passed entirely out of the hands of the Scribner organization. The remaining owners reincorporated as The Century Company, and *Scribner's Monthly* was by agreement renamed the *Century Magazine*. Under the terms of the sale of the stock, Charles Scribner's Sons agreed to stay out of the magazine business for five years.

Judging from what happened later, it would seem that they kept a careful account of the time.

The next decisive step taken by CS II had to do with the textbook business. Beginning in the 1850s the firm had built up a solid and well-known list of school books, but this part of the business was becoming more and more specialized, perhaps too much so for what was primarily a trade house. In any case, in 1883 Scribners announced the sale of its entire list of school books to Ivison, Blakeman, Taylor & Co., then one of the largest educational houses in the United States.

Thus within four years of taking over, CS II had pruned the firm drastically. But he was by nature a builder, and one could be sure that when a part of the business had to be lost or torn down, he had already begun to think about how something much bigger and much better could be set up in its place. (The new educational department that was started ten years after the sale of the old one is a good case in point.) In 1884 CS II's younger brother Arthur Hawley Scribner (A. H.) graduated from Princeton and came into the firm to help him. The two brothers worked together in a partnership for almost fifty years.

The firm benefited by what pruning had been done, for the remaining parts flowered as never before. Many of the American authors it introduced are now famous. There was H. C. Bunner, whose first book of poems, *Airs from Arcady and Elsewhere*, came out in 1884 in an edition of fifteen hundred copies. This would not seem overpessimistic even now, for the sale of poetry has not kept pace with other things. George Washington Cable first appeared in print in *Scribner's Monthly* with the short story "'Sieur George" (1873). Six years later several such pieces were collected and came out as the beloved *Old Creole Days*. Another cherished connection was Thomas

Nelson Page, whose book *In Ole Virginia* was the first of many about the South.

Lest it be thought that the firm was only the literary heir of the Confederacy, I hasten to add some names from other parts of the country. There was Henry Adams, whose *History of the United States* was published in 1889 in nine volumes and whose ironical letters to the firm are a model for any "difficult" author. Henry van Dyke, "poet, preacher, author, university teacher, diplomat" (to quote the *Dictionary of American Biography*), started out on the Scribner list with a pamphlet entitled *The National Sin of Literary Piracy* (1888). Not a very promising beginning, but the collected works of this versatile and very popular author were later to make up a set of eighteen volumes.

Three famous children's books of that period were Edward Eggleston's *Hoosier School-Boy* (1883), Howard Pyle's *The Merry Adventures of Robin Hood* (1883), and Frances Hodgson Burnett's *Little Lord Fauntleroy* (1886). Stevenson first appeared on the list with *A Child's Garden of Verses* (1885). It is interesting to note that an edition of this book (with pictures by Jessie Willcox Smith) was one of the original titles in the "Scribner Illustrated Classics." There were to be many other great English writers published by the firm: Barrie, George Meredith, Kenneth Grahame, John Galsworthy, and Winston S. Churchill, to name a few.

Around the time these works were appearing, ideas for a new magazine were being thought out. It was inconceivable that CS II could have been content without one. As a boy of fifteen he had started up a little comic monthly called *Merry Moments* and had had to give it up, not because it was unsuccessful but because it was too successful (from his father's point of view).

Few could have been surprised then in December of 1886 when the firm announced a new *Scribner's Magazine*. Its original editor (from 1887 to 1914) was Edward L. Burlingame, son of the American diplomat Anson Burlingame and literary advisor to Charles Scribner's Sons since 1879. Under him the magazine grew into something finer and more successful than the most hopeful would have dared to foresee. He had a green thumb. But to tell the story of *Scribner's Magazine* and cover its contribution to American literature and life for a half-century would take at least a separate article. It would include many of the same writers whose books helped build the reputation of the publishing firm, for the magazine was a double asset to Charles Scribner's Sons, not only in itself but also as a net for talent.

In 1894 the firm capped the climax of fifteen years of growth under CS II by moving into a stately new six-story building at Fifth Avenue and Twenty-first Street, designed by the well-known architect Ernest Flagg (CS II's brother-in-law). On the ground floor was a magnificent bookstore. . . .

Charles Scribner's Sons remained at this address for nineteen years (1894–1913), during which time a whole company of new authors were added to its list. Among them was Theodore Roosevelt, whose *Rough Riders* (1899) was the first of many successful books for Scribners. . . . Another lasting association was begun with the publication of a book on esthetics, *The Sense of Beauty* (1896), by a young philosophy teacher at Harvard, George Santayana. Almost forty years later Santayana produced a best-selling novel, *The Last Puritan* (1935). It would be hard to think of another philosopher equally versatile in letters. Edith Wharton's first book (written in collaboration with Ogden Codman, Jr.), *The Decoration of Houses* (1897), started a now-famous career. Not long after, two other authors made their debut: Ernest Seton-Thompson (later he reversed the surname) with *Wild Animals I Have Known* (1898) and James Huneker with *Mezzotints in Modern Music* (1899). The first book still sells strongly. Canons of music criticism are short-lived, but young readers are perennially interested in wild animals.

The turn of the century brought another cluster of famous first editions. John Fox, Jr.'s *Blue Grass and Rhododendron* appeared in 1901. Two years later Scribners published his novel *The Little Shepherd of Kingdom Come*, which was probably the biggest seller the firm ever had. . . . A different sort of novelist, Henry James, appeared on the list with *The Sacred Fount* (1901). Sadly enough, his greatest fame was to come long after his death.

The year 1913 may be taken as the natural beginning of a new chapter in the history of the firm. In that year another move was made up Fifth Avenue to a new and even larger Flagg building on Forty-eighth Street. . . . This was the third headquarters since the presidency of CS II and the scene of the last three almost equal periods in his fifty-five years with the firm (1875–1894, 1894–1913, 1913–1930).

CS II had been getting together a whole new team of young editors. There was Maxwell E. Perkins and the already well-known American poet John Hall Wheelock, two young Harvard graduates who invaded a then predominantly Princeton company but brought it great new successes by their editorial intuition and skill. Shortly afterwards Wallace Meyer accepted the position of advertising manager (a well-worn stepping stone for publishing talent). Later he became an editor, and in that capacity he helped bring into being some of the outstanding publications of Scribners. He worked with Douglas Southall Freeman in an editor-author relationship that included every book the latter wrote. Freeman prized the association so much that before his death he remarked that he wished there could be a special "Meyer Edition" of his biography of George Washington.

In 1913 CS II's only son (another Charles) graduated from Princeton and began his own career in publishing. He was a contemporary of the young men who were joining the firm, and his age gave him a ready grasp of the importance of the new writers who were beginning to appear on the scene. For another era in American literature was coming into being, and the firm's enthusiasm for this new work was to yield it a rich publishing harvest.

There was Alan Seeger, whose *Poems* came out in 1916, and four years later F. Scott Fitzgerald with his first novel, *This Side of Paradise*. Stark Young's *The Flower in Drama* appeared in 1923, and in the following years Ring Lardner's *How to Write Short Stories* (1924), James Boyd's *Drums* (1925), and John W. Thomason, Jr.'s *Fix Bayonets* (1925). Ernest Hemingway's *The Torrents of Spring* and *The Sun Also Rises* were both published in 1926. In view of his later achievements and his enduring loyalty to the firm, we shall always think of that as a year to set aside. Thomas Wolfe's *Look Homeward, Angel* came out in 1929.

Around this time, the long career of CS II was drawing to a close. In 1928 (the same year that his grandson George McKay Schieffelin joined the firm) he turned over the presidency to his brother A. H. and continued on only as chairman of the board. Happily, he lived to see the first published volumes of the *Dictionary of American Biography* (1928–1937), a work to which he had given every kind of support and which was probably the most important thing the firm had ever undertaken. In 1930 he died, and two years later A. H. died too, leaving CS III (my father) to preside alone.

It would be hard to think of a more difficult time in which to take over the management of a large publishing house. The

Great Depression was in its worst stage, and the future must have appeared most uncertain for books. Yet the firm continued to look for fresh talent and to take chances on new authors in a way that marks this as one of the most enterprising periods in all its history. That testifies to the aims and courage of CS III and to the devoted support his associates gave him. In the following years there appeared not only important new works by already-established authors but also the first books of many then relatively unknown writers who were later to become famous. Among these new authors were Marcia Davenport (*Mozart*, 1932), Nancy Hale (*The Young Die Good*, 1932), Marjorie Kinnan Rawlings (*South Moon Under*, 1933), Hamilton Basso (*Beauregard*, 1933), Taylor Caldwell (*Dynasty of Death*, 1938), and Christine Weston (*Be Thou the Bride*, 1940).

The years preceding World War II also saw the growth of a new Children's Book Department under the gifted editorial direction of Alice Dalgliesh. . . . Miss Dalgliesh joined Scribners in 1934, already experienced as an editor and well-known as an author. Under her there was built up title by title the most distinguished list of children's books in our history. With a sure grasp of what is fresh and valuable in the work of new writers and new artists, Miss Dalgliesh introduced a whole company of now famous names like Genevieve Foster, Katherine Milhous, Marcia Brown, and Leo Politi. Her own books, too, have brought the firm many honors and successes.

In the early fifties the firm was doing very well indeed. A number of our most successful books had just been published, and there were many promising new titles in prospect. Then quite suddenly and at a comparatively early age CS III died of a heart attack in February of 1952. He had lived to read in the manuscript Ernest Hemingway's now classic novella *The Old Man and the Sea*, and later the author dedicated the book to him and Maxwell Perkins. CS III left behind two grandsons of CS II in the business: George McKay Schieffelin and myself.*

The remainder of our story does not seem to belong so much to the realm of history as to current events. As a firm we believe strongly in the future of books and book publishing. We only hope that in this field we can play as constructive a part in our time as our predecessors did in theirs.

---

*Although, to be consistent, I should be enumerated "CS IV," I have always used the simpler "Jr." and my eldest son (the *fifth* Charles), in turn, became "III." This silent recycling of numerals inevitably causes generational confusion, but the alternative sounds too much like the Bourbon kings.

Index

Printed in the United States
By Bookmasters